10 Lessons for
Living #LocationFree

An insider's guide to living and
working anywhere and everywhere

K A T E   E M M E R S O N

First published in 2020

QuickShift Publishing
PO Box 698, Melville
Johannesburg 2109

Text copyright © Kate Emmerson
Publisher: QuickShift Publishing
Cover Illustrator: Shannan Taylor
Designer: Megan Barber Designs
Copy editor: Sean Fraser
Proof reader: Jennifer Cole
Photographer: Filmalter

Print edition ISBN: 978-0-620-90868-9

DISCLAIMER

Embarking on a life that is #LocationFree is exhilarating. Please ensure that you have all the legalities in place for travelling and working globally and stay above board when it comes to tax. Stay safe while you #LiveLightLiveLarge.

Connect with Kate Emmerson

Stay up to date with Kate's adventures and conversations with other Global Nomads on https://kate-emmerson.com/blog/
Facebook.com/kate.emmerson.page
Instagram @kate_emmerson
Linkedin.com/in/kateemmerson

Kate coaches business owners and other folk living #LocationFree, and mentors writers around the world. She lovingly cracks the whip, both online and face to face. She hosts retreats in idyllic locations strategically designed to take you offline and experience the real power of letting go.

Other published titles by Kate:

- *Clear Your Clutter*
- *Ditch Your Glitch*
- *Shift Your Home*
- *Write Your Book in 100 Days* (with Sarah Bullen and Tessa Graham)

To purchase Kate's other books, visit her Amazon profile on https://www.amazon.com/-/e/B015LPMEFC

Dedication

THIS BOOK IS DEDICATED TO every stranger I have met en route. The kindness you have shown reinforces the magic of showing up and trusting. Thank you for an ever-expanding circle where strangers become global friends. Namaste.

Contents

Introduction

Wherever you go, go with all your heart.
– Confucius

THERE WILL BE ALWAYS BE a reason to say no. An excuse to stay within the realm of the known. To stay put and pretend you don't *really* want to follow that dream. To relinquish the freedom you crave in favour of the safety of security. But at what cost?

It takes courage to step beyond the everyday, the norm, to go against the grain of what's expected of you in terms of your responsibilities. Yet, in my experience, there is also a global movement towards doing things differently: working remotely, going off grid, living in bio-communities, taking things slower or simply living our own version of a well-curated life. Advancements in technology have freed up so many industries, and of course 2020 forced everyone to rethink all our preconceptions – and fast! While some of us may be desperate for things to return to "normalcy", to a "life before", I think we are poised for a wonderful shift in the way we view the world and, in particular, our own lives. What if this is the precise moment to change how we live, what we say yes to and how we honour the fact that life is so short?

We need to live our life well! We have to be willing to leap into that space that is a brilliant and passionate life. I have been inspiring, coaching, de-cluttering and speaking on stage internationally for

17 years, helping clients live their best lives and step up to attain their goals. My motto is #LiveLightLiveLarge and the bulk of my work centres around helping clients let go, make space, get organised, release the past and follow their heart. My heart skips a beat at the opportunity to travel, to explore, and to experience new places, encounter new faces and connect deeply with people. I too needed to step up to my own version of a life lived on the "next level" and face my next challenge, a new adventure and find my passion on a global stage.

If you are on the verge of de-cluttering your life, drastically downsizing, and yearn to live in different countries while working globally, then you will find yourself nodding and being inspired by these pages. My aim is to help answer the questions whirling in your mind, allay your fears and help you find the solutions to get you started on your journey.

I can hardly believe that my initial idea – wild as it was – of packing up and living #LocationFree for just one year has magically turned into five! Beyond the first few months after I set out, I honestly didn't know much, had no idea where I would end up. Yes, I had lined up some big international talks and booked retreat work from January until June but then … wide-open space and a world of possibility! It was a heady mix – one part exciting, one part terrifying and a dash of crazy!

This book shares five years of living #LocationFree. Here I share an insider's view on what location-free living is truly all about. And, in order to give you a more diverse perspective, I realised it would be useful to interview others I met along the way – men and women, single and married, with different forms of work or business, who share insights and ideas, highs and lows.

There are so many ways to curate this lifestyle; there is no single, rigid version. You can conjure up any version you wish and I hope that we are able to help you take the leap. Those who share their experiences here range in age from "midlife" to 60, but what they have in common is that they have been brave and crazy enough to follow their deepest calling, each living their own version of the Global Nomad lifestyle.

I feel so privileged that you have this book in your hand – let's get started on inspiring new possibilities. Are you ready to take the plunge?

How to use this book

This book follows 10 lessons that help us think about, pre-empt, prepare and ace all aspects of living #LocationFree. You can start at the beginning and work through these pages step by step, or jump straight ahead to the section you need to get to grips with first.

To stay up to date with their lifestyle, be sure to reach out and connect with me and all the others featured here. Start your global community today – all contact details appear in the biographies listed at the back of the book.

This book has one aim: to share as much as possible of what it's really like and how to get the most from a global lifestyle. It will open your eyes and heart to help you to take the plunge.

LESSON

1

Embracing the
#LocationFree mindset

L OOKING BACK ON YOUR LIFE, you can probably pinpoint one pivotal
moment that turned out to be a life-changing decision for you.
Even though it may have meant that any number of complex events
had to converge and intertwine in order for you get you there, they
still had to reach that point at that particular time in that order.
How you react and respond in that instant makes all the difference.
Deeply inspired ideas can pop into your consciousness in a flash.
The question is: will you listen or will you bow to the nagging voice
of fear in that nanosecond of *What if?* It was a simple statement that
opened the door to my new way of life. "We're getting a divorce
and we cannot afford to stay on this property any longer. I'm sorry,
Kate, but we have to be out the house, and that includes you in the
treehouse. In two months!"

"Oh … Oh, gosh. I'm so, so sorry to hear that … and … yes, of course, no problem at all," I replied, a tremble in my voice. But internally – *Bam!* – a lightning bolt zapped my heart.

I had just returned from a three-week trip abroad with my partner and mum. We had travelled to Las Vegas to attend a glamorous red-carpet premiere of *The Secrets of the Keys*, a film I had featured in. I had appeared alongside the world's leading experts on self-development and was riding high on the possibilities of life. By then, I had already been living something of a global lifestyle, travelling extensively for up to six months of the previous two years. I was working a lot in the international arena, delivering keynote talks, running retreats, hosting Mastermind workshops, as well as facilitating most of my coaching work online. This was long before Covid19 got every business and granny in slippers on Zoom – I had been coaching and mentoring online since 2005.

My business was expanding fast, gaining traction as South Africa's clutter expert, a best-selling author and traveller extraordinaire. I already had my sights set on leaving South Africa to live in another country. I am no stranger to global travel. My first experience was at three years old, when I boarded a postal ship that brought me and my family from the UK to South Africa; my next travel adventure saw me flying solo across the country at the age of eight. As a teenager I took a month-long trip to improve my French with Madame Hardy, followed by a six-week year-end jaunt to Europe, halfway through my degree to gather energy to finish my BA degree. And at 21 I left South Africa to work and travel abroad.

Having shared my #LiveLightLiveLarge motto for years, as I took in the words of my landlady, I knew that the time had come … It was time to lean in, dive deeper and live my own motto with honesty and intent. It was time to let go.

In the very instant I stuttered, "No problem," I knew that I could not – would not – create yet another nest in Johannesburg. It had never been my chosen long-term home; six years prior, after my life had taken a really bad nose dive, both personally and professionally, I had returned for financial reasons. That journey was detailed in my book *Ditch Your Glitch*. By this point, however, I knew I had already been living in the City of Gold for too long. I felt I was being eaten up and losing the deeper connection with my soul.

Even on the back of all my local and international travelling to get out the city, up until that very moment, standing in my treehouse, I guess I had still called Johannesburg home. It was where I came to rest after travelling and where Stripey, my four-pawed friend, always waited patiently for me at the gate. At the time of this lightning-bolt moment, I had a gorgeous treehouse home (which is what I called my wonderful apartment in Greenside looking straight onto a purple expanse of jacaranda), a beloved cat, a fully paid-off car, incredible friends, a successful business, massive network – and a beautiful man I had been dating for an incredible eight months. And yet, in a flash of clear, calm knowing, I knew I was going to pack up and finally stop calling Johannesburg "home."

It was time for the next level.
Time to pack up my home.
To use this sign as a real opportunity.
To live location free for a year.
To actively seek out the next step.
It was terrifying and exhilarating all at once.

I scanned my beautiful studio apartment looking directly onto the famous lilac jacaranda trees that create carpets of purple, my beautiful art, the white trestle table where I had written two books, and all my books and objet d'art on my bookshelves. I perused my life that lay sprawled out in front of me, and just knew it was "done", over, certainly in the form it had been until this moment. Rapidly, I started calculating what I might keep. Knowing that I was about to embrace one year of living entirely location free, while still trying to figure out what the next step might be, I hardly slept.

That night, as I tossed and turned, I coined a term for this next phase of my life: #TheMinimalistManifesto.

There were two immediate hurdles to face – My Cat and My Man. It was clear that the next step was to share my decision with my partner … It wasn't entirely out of the blue. From the moment we had met, exactly one year before at a salsa party, he already knew that my sights were set on living abroad. I didn't have all the answers or know all the steps, so there was little more I could do then other than bravely share my decision with him. Next was a call to a dear friend to talk about the possibility of Stripey living with them for a year?

It was already the end of November, and I was still up to my ears in work. I had the Johannesburg premiere of *The Secrets of the Keys* to pull off just one week after landing from Vegas. There would be 100 VIP clients, guests and media attending my own red-carpet event, and yet I knew instinctively that I wanted my move to happen even sooner than the end-January D-day. Less than two months later, on 25 January 2016, the plan unfolded rapidly. The first step was to move Stripey to his new home with my friend up the road, where he would have three human bodies and another kitty to snuggle and love.

Then I packed my three – yes, *three!* – boxes and one large piece of art into the car of another dear friend to store in his garage. Mmmm … yes, the irony of storing *anything* in someone else's garage is not lost on me, the de-clutter Deva, but apart from one large piece of art that was wrapped up separately, those three boxes held my entire life:

- one box had been allocated solely to five years' worth of legal records and tax documents for my South African-based business (I always recommend you stay legal!),
- another housed two of my Nan's handmade patchwork quilts and my long-time teddy Francesca, and
- the third held my precious objet d'art and favourite, smaller framed art.

This was the sum total of my precious stuff, which would find its way to me wherever I decided home was one day in the future.

Next, the car dealer arrived, showing transfer of ownership along with proof of payment as he collected my funky Peugeot Cabriolet. Oh, how I loved driving with that top down and the music blaring, and I knew how much fun the next owner would have in it too!

Lastly, my partner picked me up, and drove me and my two suitcases to his home across town to crack open a bottle of wine.

Already living as a minimalist with a beautiful yet uber-practical "capsule wardrobe", I had still managed to reduce it by passing clothes and shoes onto others who would be able to make better use of them. Everything I kept fitted into two suitcases: one large one weighing 23 kilograms for long-haul check-in flights, and the other to accompany me as hand luggage. Simple, compact and living *light*.

At my partner's home, I didn't unpack my stuff, but placed my two suitcases in his spare room and lived out of them whenever I visited. My clothes were always beautifully packed, like those you would find in a high-end store, which made it easy for outfit choices. I could see at a glance everything I owned neatly "rolded" in my suitcase. To share my lifestyle and showcase my cleverly packed suitcase, I was even interviewed live by presenter Jeannie D of *The Expresso Show*, one of South Africa's premiere TV shows. So it was that I found myself on national television, my suitcase on display for all to see, knickers and all!

Just two days after vacating my treehouse and heading across town for that celebratory bottle of wine, I left for Durban for my first keynote talk of the year. And so began the reality of living #LocationFree. My mind was clear, my heart wide open and my excitement levels off the chart.

I knew right from the outset that living #LocationFree for one year would be easy as pie for me, but as that first year drew rapidly to a close, I knew a second year was on the cards. I was having a ball – and here we are, five years down the line from that lightning-bolt moment.

To be honest, even though I was really enjoying gallivanting around the world, revelling in my numerous adventures and flying high with business, I was totally winging it … and I still am! That's another reward of this lifestyle – that you can make it up as you go along, right? Yes, but that doesn't mean it's always easy or plain sailing, though.

I think the one issue I felt unsure about, one that was alarmingly unsettling for me, was how Johannesburg and South Africa would realistically unfold moving forward.

- How would my partner and I navigate our committed life together?
- How and where would we see each other?
- How would I factor in work commitments in South Africa among extended global travel?

I was already travelling for more than six months in the year and I now wanted to increase that to nine months. My idea was to return for specific work commitments and to build my relationship. This move meant that I no longer considered Johannesburg my official base. My base was honestly wherever I was at that moment.

Because my partner was based in Johannesburg, however, I ensured I visited at least three or four times annually, and he did his best to make one annual trip to travel with me. Some years were easier than others in terms of the time we managed to carve out for each other.

Part of the challenge of the #LocationFree mindset is fielding the questions, especially the cocktail party conversations.

"So … where do you live?"

"I live everywhere and nowhere … around the world, location free. I don't have a permanent home base."

There would be a slight gasp or an awkward silence, inevitably followed by some version of the following:

"What do you mean you don't have a home?"

"Yes, but where do you actually *live*?"

"What about your friends?"

"Aren't you lonely?"

"Did your business collapse?"

"What are you running away from?"

"Are you sick?"

"Where do you pay tax?"

"Where do you sleep?"

"Kate, where do you call home? *Where*?"

"I don't understand this …"

"I could *never* do that!"

"That's just crazy! What do you mean? Where do you go *back* to?"

But I would simply flash my cheekiest grin and say, "I'm not homeless – I am simply running my business location free. I live wherever I am."

If I was in Greece, Greece was my home. In the USA, then that was home. Wherever I lay my suitcases, computer and toothbrush … that was home.

I was living the dream I had conjured up a long time ago. When I first qualified as a professional life coach in the United Kingdom back in 2003, my dream was to be able to sit on a mountain and coach clients anywhere in the world. That was always the vision. Tangible and real – feeding into my love of adventure, travel and a well-lived, passionate life. Even when all I had at my disposal were old-fashioned landlines, dial-up internet, Skype or such like, I had always offered clients the online option of working with me. That is also what motivated me to start writing my first online coaching courses back in 2004.

Are you deeply terrified or ecstatically enthralled at the prospect of this for yourself? Perhaps a mixture? Unless you are a millennial tech worker where it's the norm to work online from a beach, for instance, this not a well-documented lifestyle choice for those of us over 40. A lot of my time and work has been educating people about my lifestyle of choice – which is precisely why I am sharing this with you!

My partner and I never fully discussed, or perhaps never completely understood all the ins and outs of this arrangement. My original plan – in as much as there was any "plan" – was that I would only be in Johannesburg for about a month at a time. So, in essence, I wasn't moving *in* with him, nor was I leaving any stuff at his place. Although we were still in a deeply committed relationship, I was there when I was there, and not when I wasn't. Details of this arrangement changed and morphed over the years. There were times when I spent longer stretches in Johannesburg, perhaps for extended work over Women's Month, to visit and care for him when he was having a major operation, or longer over festive seasons when our respective families visited. From the outset, it felt as clear as it needed to be. I was, after all, needing to feel my way around and *live* into the lifestyle. To learn what worked and what didn't.

You can't always know all the steps at the outset, can you? We may not take that leap if we knew ahead of time what might be thrown at us en route. Are you up for that challenge in your life yet, or are you perhaps playing it all a little too safe? I hope that by the time you have read more of my story and what others have to say, that you too will be inspired to at least try this for yourself. Or, if you are already doing it, that you will find a way to embrace it even deeper and allow yourself to be immersed in the joy of the unknown.

Over time, I gained some clarity, of course, specifically around the words "home" and "back". Even though my business and tax was still based in South Africa until 2020, I was no longer calling the country *home*. It was simply South Africa. On that very first January in 2016, travelling to Durban for that talk, I started referring to my escapades as travelling *to* rather than *from* somewhere. It would have been easy for me to say I was returning to Durban, because that is where I had grown up. Instead, I started educating, asking, begging my friends and clients to not ask, "Kate, when are you coming *home*? When are you *back* in South Africa?"

Every time I "returned" to a place, I would do my best to simply say, "I am going to ..." – wherever that "to" happened to be. That was an energetic mindset shift for me.

The concept of "going back" felt old school, heavy, stuck, past, and all about one traditional home base. This new lifestyle and the mindset I needed to embrace were about living light, living free, about movement and energy. And so, as I coined the phrase #TheMinimalistManifesto, I started immersing in and living the life.

And now, five years down the line, the time has come to look at it retrospectively. At first I thought it was to make sense of it all for me, to gain some perspective on what, why and how – what I had gained and what I had lost along the way. The honest and raw reality of what it has been like. After all, nothing is what it seems from the outside looking in.

Maybe you are looking for a nudge, or perhaps permission to do this for yourself? If so, I do my best to share a vulnerable and honest account of living #LocationFree for five years. I also draw on other fabulous souls who agreed to share their personal stories, insights, lessons and tips. That way, you get a more rounded view of what this lifestyle is really like – from the inside, not the glam Instagram version. I hope it helps you say yes, even if for a short while, to experience the freedom.

If you choose this way of life, do so with your eyes wide open, your heart ready to explode and immerse yourself into a life worth living.

Introducing some amazing folk

While I refer to this lifestyle as #LocationFree and living #TheMinimalistManifesto, I'd love to introduce you to some incredible individuals and how they refer to it. At the end of each chapter, they share their own insights and tips. Based all over the world, from different countries and cultures, we share what it means to live our own version of #LocationFree.

My partner, Jill, and I are "Nomadic Artists". We both create physical and digital art; I also have been doing tattoos for over 20 years. As much as possible, we paint murals in exchange for accommodation, and sometimes food, wherever we travel. We've been living this lifestyle for two and a half years.

—Chris de Cap

Work-wise, I have been location independent for 13 years. I spent one and a half years of this living the Digital Nomad lifestyle in South-East Asia and Central America. Although I'm Dutch, I now live in the Canary Islands, and my laptop joins me wherever I travel.

—André Gussekloo

I've been working for myself since 2002. Although I've been working while travelling since then, I began to really think of it as "Remote Working" in February 2017 when I went on a trip with "Unsettled". Since then, I've been spending about three to four months a year away from New York City, mostly in the winter.

—Uday Jhunjhunwala

The term that resonates most is "Location Independent". I started living this way at the end of 2017. The Digital Nomad movement was in full swing and I thought it was geared more towards the younger millennial traveller, so I wasn't sure I could make the lifestyle work for me. I knew I wanted more freedom and also to meet other entrepreneurs who were a similar age to me so I could expand my network and also my professional experience.

—**Victoria Jane Watson**

I refer to it as "Remote Working/Digital Nomad". I have been travelling a lot with my work for quite some years, but since July 2017 without a steady residence.

—**Nabila Welk**

"Freedom of Lifestyle" has been my number-one attribute since a very young age. To me, it means I always have the opportunity to say no and able to work to my own rhythm rather than someone else's routine. It means I can travel and explore. It means I can be authentically me.

—**Lynne Scullard**

I refer to myself as "Globally Shifting Performance" and I have been contracted and living internationally since September 2019.

—**Deborah Louise Botha**

I've been on the road since late 2016. I don't really refer to it as "Location Free", "Global Nomad", any of those terms. However, when I meet people during travelling, they tend to say, "Oh, you must be one of those Digital Nomads." So I find that outside of these circles of people that work online and live anywhere, that people tend to categorise them as digital nomads. I just consider myself to be someone who doesn't live in their home country and who goes from country to country based on how I feel and that my income is primarily derived through online means and is not tied to any specific location.

—*Gene Ellis*

I usually just say I live "House-less"; I don't really use a term for it. I have been living this way for close to four years now. The first two years I mainly did house- (and pet-) sitting, all over Europe, for stretches of three weeks to three months. The last one and a half to two years, due to the health situation of my parents, I have been gradually doing fewer and shorter housesitting stays, and staying with my parents and supporting them the rest of the time. Recently we have started receiving more professional aid for their situation, so I'm looking forward to slowly returning to the more spacious situation of the first two years.

—Martin van den Berg

I call myself a "Nomad". I have never liked being in one place too long. I have been travelling alone since I was 19, on and off throughout my life. In 2015 I tried to be away from Denmark for three months in winter – three different countries – and I loved it. So I sold most of my stuff, gave the rest away and moved to Tenerife, where I lived for one year to see if my wings could carry me. They could, so in November 2018 I went to Colombia and have been on the road ever since, never more than one month in one place.

—Mette Glargaard

I've been very intentional in my way of working and living. I get bored easily and I'm super curious about the world so I gave myself the option to always have Base Camp One in the UK and the option to pack two bags and whizz off somewhere. My first big adventure started as a two-week holiday to Malaga and I ended up staying there. I secretly knew I was going to stay because I'd set my life and business up to do this. I put zero pressure on myself to stay or come home and felt my way through the transition. So far, it's been a blast!

—Carolynne Alexander

I'm a "Location Free Digital Nomad and Remote Worker". I live mostly between two countries (Spain and Finland), but I've also worked from other locations while on the road, travelling or making holiday. I work from the airports when travelling. I can work from wherever with a reliable internet connection: my "office" is a laptop, phone and a notebook. If it wasn't for my child, I would travel [or] change locations more often. We live winters in Spain and summers in Finland. In between, I sometimes take trips somewhere else. My customers are in Finland and my work is continuous no matter where I am. Most of my contracts are long, for years, so I don't have to be hunting new customers all the time.

—Katia Enbuske

Since February 2019 I have been living as a "Digital Nomad", travelling around the world and working from various places.

—Jan van Kuijk

I guess I would call myself a "Portable Professional". I'm currently living in Santiago in Chile. I don't necessarily see it as my permanent place in the sun, but it is where I am for now. The by-line is that I will go wherever the work is, because I have no family commitments and so I'm available to go and work wherever the project needs me to be. Most of my work I do via technology, my clients are outside of Chile and so I guess in that sense I'm a remote Virtual Coach.

—Michelle Clarke

I tend to call myself an "Intentional Nomad" - it could depend on who I'm talking to. Some family and friends call me a gypsy. I don't have anything hard and fast that I actually call it. I've been on the road since 4 July 2015. I remember that quite specifically because the fourth of July is, of course, Independence Day in America and it was the day that I left my marriage and the family home for the last time. So it was like my own

Independence Day. So 4 July every year is my kind of anniversary and it'll be six years this coming fourth of July.

—**Dee Brooks**

I've been a self-employed virtual assistant since 2010 and consider myself a "Digital Nomad" as hubby Rob and I have been living a freedom lifestyle, travelling Europe with our pets since September 2017. I can work from anywhere with good internet connection and, so far, have lived in 12 different homes in two and a half years. As we were travelling with two dogs, I needed to book homes with adequate outside space, so the cheaper apartments were not an option. Therefore, we often stayed in houses too large for just Rob and I because they had a garden! We also missed staying in town, in walking distance of shops and bars, as most houses with land tended to be in the countryside. We had seen very few places in Europe, and as this was a lifestyle choice; it was an adventure to stay in places that would not normally be on our "to visit" list.

—**Nancy Benn**

 **TOP TIPS!**

- Listen to the rumbling in your heart, whether that is a lightning-flash moment or multiple small nudges.
- Choose a motto or quote to ensure that your *why* stays top of mind. Mine is #LiveLightLiveLarge.
- Learn to shift your language around your lifestyle in a way that feels empowering and inspirational.

LESSON

2

Taking the plunge

LET'S BE HONEST, LIVING ##LocationFree might push some buttons! One of the most important reasons I wrote this book was to help others closer to my midlife age bracket find the courage to do so too. Unless you are a descendant of a nomadic tribe from the Sahara or have Romanian gypsy blood running through your veins, it requires a leap of faith. Or perhaps you are in your twenties and seeing (uhm … drinking?) the world wide-eyed, footloose and fancy free for the first time. If not, living #LocationFree will probably be met with some incredulity, astonishment, disdain and lots of strange looks.

One of the hardest things to manage when you plunge into this way of life is *other* people. Their questions, comments, preconceived judgments. I once heard that a client had commented to my business partner: "Well, if Kate is living out of a suitcase, then I don't know whether I really want to work with her – she clearly isn't successful!"

Mmm … To be honest, though, that comment did serve as a point of reflection and make me stop for a moment. To think about perceptions and what others think. I did take time to sit with that and wonder if I was damaging my brand? Was I? Can we ever know the impact of a significant decision? I had worked super hard to create and build a trusted personal brand, was pretty well known in South Africa, and had sustained long-standing clients around the world.

My life's work, passion and brand message is all centred around "#livelightlivelarge – to have less, need less, be more, experience more. All about de-cluttering and letting go. But had I taken it too far? It's a valid question, right?

- Was it unsettling for some folk?
- Did long-standing clients need me to be in South Africa?
- Did it inspire people or terrify them?
- Did it perhaps make them trust me less?
- Or was the opposite of all that potentially true too?

I had to remind myself that I had chosen to take the plunge, and how other people responded was really none of my business. My happiness and choices were my responsibility alone. So, while I appreciated that that comment offered a point of reflection for me, I chose to let it go and move on. I was, after all, having the time of my life … Well, most of the time anyway – it's not all glamour and gloss, of course.

I guess I hadn't been educating people enough about what it meant for me. The truth is that in the past five years of living #LocationFree I have accomplished *more* than in the previous 10 years. I have written another three books, trebled my business, taken most of the last year off, worked virtually *no* weekends (my default norm in the past), and travelled the globe. I even earned more in one week than I billed in some years and crossed the six-figure mark. I paid of all debt, celebrated turning 50, sold off the IP to my online coaching courses, helped hundred of authors write their own books and deepened friendships around the world. I was also in a committed relationship for four of the five years living #LocationFree.

But we do need to be able sit back and take stock … And there have been many, many WTF moments – one cannot escape them:
- a feeling of deep loneliness,
- the cloak of depression – deep, dark holes of it,
- processing grief and loss,
- longing for my partner,
- experiencing complete exhaustion and adrenal burnout,
- physical pain from travelling too much, and
- sometimes, ironically, missing a full-time base to nest.

I think every one of us on this planet has to live with the pros and cons of any life we choose. None of us can escape that. We each have to decide what are our absolute non-negotiables to help us live the best version of our lives.

One of the very first things I suggest you be crystal clear on is your *why*. What is this lifestyle and journey all about for you?
- Is it to be solo or with your family?
- Is going on this adventure to keep a relationship together?
- Is it to heal and find your real self again after a break-up or divorce?
- Is it about searching for your next forever home and staying open about where that might be?
- Is it purely about adventure and experiencing life to the full?
- Is it about seeing how little "stuff" you really need to be happy?
- Is it a time-specific adventure, like an adult version of the gap year?
- Is it only for the foreseeable future, or with an aim to "live" in 10 different countries over five years?

In the end, all that matters, however, is that *you* know *your* why! It is your why that will ease you through the tougher aspects.

Note: If your aim is simply to avoid tax and fly under the radar for all things legal and required, this book is really *not* for you!

You also need to know upfront that your nearest and dearest, those closest to you, might give you the hardest time about this idea. They might not understand, let alone be fully supportive. Just because you want to take the plunge doesn't mean they will approve of it. They might struggle to understand and get behind your dreams, particularly if they have a very different outlook, or are committed to a lifestyle that is worlds away from what you are looking for for yourself. You choosing to go after something exciting, challenging, new and off the wall may require them to reflect on their own lives, to look at life and its options from a different perspective.

It's usually far easier for others to say, "Are you mad? You can't do that! You cannot sell your home, leave your well-paying job, sell your car, blah-blah-blah ..."

Of course, often what others say gives voice to the niggling ones in our own head. That, however, comes back to reflection and how you navigate the fears you might face.

It's much harder for observers to dare say, "Gosh, good luck! I wish I was brave enough to do this too. I'd love to sell up, pack up, take the kids out of school and go experience life." That would require willingness and openhearted courage; staying put is usually far safer and more mainstream. But if 2020's handling of Covid19 has taught us anything, it is that life is not promised, so we need to grab it by the horns.

Lower your expectations and let others be. Don't expect them to embrace your ideas or be your most robust champion. Remember that this idea might mean they no longer have you at arm's length, can't pop in for tea when they want, and simply don't know how to explain your life to themselves. It might even force them to question everything they hold sacrosanct.

You might have to follow your inner yearning, your own moral code and travel compass on your own. To dare to be bold, to carve out a life worlds away from what you know now. A life different to theirs. That's a potentially lonely path to walk.

You can't spend all your time looking for others to ratify your ideas and potential. Sometimes you have to dream it up and follow the thread. Do what you feel you want to, even when you don't have all the answers! That's okay. This book will give you a great heads up on what may be in store for you. But more than that, you have to trust *your* heart and your calling and leave all the naysayers behind. But be sure to send them colourful postcards filled with tales from exotic places.

As you contemplate taking the plunge, you will also have to get your A into G, your ducks in a row and some things super-sorted. Think of it as tackling a project: Project Plunge!

Tie things up at work and home as if you know exactly where you are going and when – even if you don't know it all right now. You might need to create detailed timelines and spreadsheets so that you gear up step by step. Perhaps you need to have specific conversations with key people in your life. Or perhaps my story resonated where I made the decision and *then* shared it? There is no right or wrong way – it's about doing what is appropriate for you.

Could you wrap up your projects, take care of the necessary admin, and start the process of downsizing how you live and begin packing up? If you need more help de-cluttering, downsizing and even selling your home, be sure to check out my other books.

Contemplating living #LocationFree and being on the move is vastly different from packing for your regular two-week holiday. You will need to organise your entire life:
- Pack everything you need for both work and play.
- Make backups of all the necessary documents, files and important papers.

- Have access to what else you might need when you need it. How, for instance, are you going to store things you decide to keep in the long term?
- Perhaps you will do seasonal wardrobe swops and make use of modern storage pods?
- Are able to keep working with as little interruption as possible?

#LocationFree does not in any way, shape or form mean responsibility free! It simply means you don't have one fixed location, one fixed workplace or a permanent physical address. It requires fluidity, flexibility and some preparedness in your approach to life, work and home.

 **WHAT OTHERS SAY ABOUT ...**

Taking the plunge

The "lightning-bolt" moment, as Jill calls it, happened the night of 11 January 2017, when she was working on some art in her office/studio. She had the documentary Minimalism playing as she worked, and it dawned on her that the thing keeping us from travelling was all this stuff.

She walked into the living room, sat down beside me and asked, "Can we talk?" I braced for some kind of horrible thing to be discussed and said, "Sure. What do you want to talk about?" She took a deep breath and asked, "What if we sold everything, and just went travelling?"

My first reaction was, "What about the plants?"

I was also a landscaper at the time, and had been carting a large number of plants in pots with me to various different places I lived for the previous five years. When I hooked up with Jill, I started actually planting them in her yard. Her yard was a large grass rectangle, with no gardens when I stepped foot there. The property was a garden oasis by the time we left.

"We can live in places where all sorts of plants grow," she explained.

"But what about my tattoo shop?" I asked. I had just, within the past year, opened a tattoo shop in the town we lived.

"Fuck your tattoo shop, the world is your tattoo shop!" she exclaimed.

I sat back and thought it over for a few minutes. "Yeah, let's do this," was my reply.

Jill asked me, "Are you sure?"

"Fuck yeah, I don't think there's any possible way for us not to do this."

For the following nine months, through summer, which was the busy season for both our jobs (Jill ran a painting business), we finished creating some gardens and renovating the house, and had numerous yard sales to get rid of stuff.

We don't miss any of that stuff.

During this process we were hired for our first housesitting gig in Costa Rica, and it was then that we had a specific date and destination. Before then, all we knew was that we wanted to be somewhere warm by winter. We left Canada on 14 October 2017.

—Chris de Cap

I'd always had the dream to work Location Free. I've had multiple styles of business. Some were not able to be location free, but this time round it was my vision to do it and I pulled it off! It was only when the right opportunity presented itself that I took it, so it was half intentional and half opportunity.

—Carolynne Alexander

I came to Chile for a three-month sabbatical after the death of my father. My father was a great traveller and he really encouraged me to travel up beyond South Africa, which I did many times. I've travelled a lot. But he was like, "Go and live somewhere else." When he died, I thought that was great advice. I chose to come to a region of the world where I didn't need to get a travel visa because with a South African passport it's quite tough. One always needs permission. Nobody declines you permission, but it's sort of a pain to get it. So I chose to come to Latin America because at that time the entire continent was open to South Africans and of all the places in Latin America or in South America at that time, Chile was most stable. So it was an easy place to navigate.

—Michelle Clarke

I guess when I discovered Unsettled, that made it really easy for me to work remotely. However, there was a moment in 2014 when I got into a freak accident that made walking, cooking and typing quite difficult. Once I recovered from that, I decided to spend even more time travelling and working from wherever I was, and by doing that I saw that there were a lot of other people doing it as well.

—Uday Jhunjhunwala

Having always had a desire to travel and teach, it started becoming a reality for me when I became the country manager for two International companies in 2013. In those two years, I was exposed to the dynamics of dealing with corporates and NPOs around the world. This evoked a love for culturally diverse training, as I could apply and share those Aha! moments that I had experienced overseas in my workshops at home. When that association ended, the desire to continue offering training and developing many varied cultures never left me. In fact, it became the hunger that gnawed at me for the next five years. In the beginning of

2019, I felt a restlessness that I could no longer contain, nor did I want to. My daughters, who are my entire world, were 27 and 22. Both were living their lives and making plans for their futures, and I realised that I was free to make life choices that were a bit more "me centred". My youngest, who is currently working on ships, came home after her first contract and, in sharing her stories, her growth, the challenges that crew life offers, she mentioned that I would be a good fit on the ships, because I love to learn different cultures. The seed was planted. I decided to get an internationally recognised certificate in English (TEFL) as I believed that might help. The rest was history, and within a few weeks, I had been head hunted by a UK agency. Within two weeks of being offered the position, I was required to be in Miami for an HR conference. There was no time to second-guess this opportunity – it had been brewing for five years. I was laser focused in packing up my small apartment, rehoming my beautiful girly cat Phoebe, driving across borders to get my USA visa, police clearance and the very expensive medical required to join. Twelve days later, I boarded a plane to the USA to start what I knew was going to be my next chapter of Intentional living! The unmistakable heartbeat of travel and teaching was thumping boldly in my chest.

—Deborah Louise Botha

In terms of a defining or pivotal moment, there really wasn't one – it just naturally evolved that way. I've always been someone who travels a lot and I was starting to spend more and more time outside of the States. And so it was just gradual where I realised, "Now I'm gone for two months, now I'm gone for three months." And then at one point I said, "Okay, now I've been gone for six months and now I'm just going to stay gone a year." And during those times I was still maintaining some sort of residence back in the States. Late 2016 was the last time I had a residence back in the States.

—Gene Ellis

Rob and I had always wanted to live abroad and actually settled on Portugal. We bought an almost-ruin there and spent three years renovating the property with a view to moving out permanently by the time Rob was 50 years old. We never achieved our goal due to marital problems between 2008 and 2010, which necessitated selling our house in Portugal and our home in England, but we never lost the dream to leave the UK. In spring 2017, on a rainy day after a cold wet winter, I was watching birds on the feeder in the back garden from my home-office window when I suddenly realised I had a portable business and could be working from somewhere warmer! I didn't have to be based in our Derbyshire home, or even the UK, so we could reignite our dream to move abroad once again.

Rob and I began to explore options, researching where in the world was considered a good value place to live. We were intrigued by Uruguay and also considered Thailand and India, but didn't particularly want to put our dogs through the hassle of a flight. I was also afraid to move so far from our loved ones and into a totally different culture. I was adventurous, but only to a point! Therefore, we decided to be a little more practical, stay closer to home and use our car to drive around Europe. As we "knew" Portugal, we decided to initially head there before moving on, eastwards through the rest of Europe.

—Nancy Benn

It developed over the years until in July 2017 I had to leave my flat in which I had been living for nine years. I decided not to rent anything steady for a while and I have been living Location Free for three years now.

—Nabila Welk

I have always had a different sense of time. This was evident when I had my first formal job as a junior computer programmer. I would think of ideas or solutions at 4 am and you'd find me in the office at 5 am implementing them.

Discovering I had a preference for working with people rather than machinery, I moved into sales. I then reported to my boss's father who thought that if your jacket hung at the back of your chair then you were working. He expected my jacket to be there from 8 am to 5 pm. N.A.F.!

As I had the top sales in the organisation, I felt confident to approach my boss and say no. I asked him to address it with his father and he did. In every subsequent job I've had I have managed to work in my own time, even in large corporates. In saying no to those routines, I said yes to my freedom.

I have been managing my own companies remotely for over two years now.

—**Lynne Scullard**

My first shift was from employee to freelance writer, after which it occurred to me that I could basically work from anywhere, as long as I had an internet connection. Reading The 4-Hour Work Week (Tim Ferris) back in 2008 was one pivotal moment in the way I viewed my work/life balance. I remember googling for 4HWW business ideas and coming across these guys living the Digital Nomad lifestyle in Thailand. I thought – I'd love to try that too!

—**André Gussekloo**

At the time, I was living in London and was starting to feel like I needed to shake things up. I had known for a couple of years that I wanted to potentially move to Spain, but at the time it felt like it was a big move so I decided to seek out an organised trip that would give me a "taste" of being location independent and then eventually moving abroad.

I came across a company called Unsettled who organises co-working retreats and applied for their 30-day experience in Porto, Portugal. It felt like something clicked and I knew this trip was going to be the beginning of a whole new chapter for me.

—Victoria Jane Watson

After I left a job quite frustrated, I decided to take a year off (sabbatical) to travel and get rid of my frustrations and consequent health issues.

I started with a two-month volunteering period at a Buddhist centre in Ireland, after which the idea was to book a round the world trip and go travelling. However, I was so exactly where I needed to be at the Buddhist centre that those two months turned into 15 months, after which I travelled for another nine months in Spain, volunteering and attempting to better my Spanish language skills.

After this time, I returned to the Netherlands and found a pretty good job at the height of the recession, which was pretty amazing. But within a week of this job, I realised that I no longer fit this life - driving on the highway where everyone tries to get a place ahead at the cost of somebody else, to get to a desk where I spend eight-plus hours sitting behind a computer doing things I literally cared nothing for, only to get back on the highway to a house that no longer felt like home.

After this realisation, it still took me a year and a half to actually "get out", as I wanted to give my employers time to find a suitable replacement, and needed time myself to do up and sell my house and get rid of most of my stuff, etcetera. But that first week on the job would have been the most pivotal moment, together with the moment of being told about the Buddhist centre, and following my gut to actually go there. That opened my eyes to the fact that there are other options than the life society has laid out for us.

—Martin van den Berg

There were several. But I asked myself after a breakup, "If I could do anything with my life, what would I do?" and the answer was clear: "Be on a constant adventure in the world."

—Mette Glargaard

I have always been a "nomad". I left Finland when I was 18 and travelled around the world for five years, doing odd jobs along the way to finance my travels. Back then there was hardly internet and no possibilities to work long distance like nowadays. Later in life I studied in Spain for two years and went back to Finland with a great business idea that kept me in Finland for almost 10 years, until I finally sold it to get more freedom of movement. At that time I had become a mother and decided with my partner that it would be a great opportunity to hit the road again. So, when our son was just seven months old, we went travelling around the world for one and half years. During that time, I had time to think of a plan how to sustain a more mobile lifestyle, and when we returned to Finland I studied a profession that would allow me to work location free. Now I'm running my accounting agency, 100% digital, which provides me with a solid monthly income. Since I'm interested in helping others to achieve their big dreams, I studied business and life coaching, which I will combine with my accounting.

It took me three years to get things to the point that the business was running smoothly, and we were able to move, again to Spain, being the southernmost area of the European Union. We needed our child to be able to attend school and, after investigating carefully different locations in the world, we felt that the smartest thing was to have the home base in a EU country (because we have EU passports).

—Katia Enbuske

Back in 2005 I took the decision to live location independent and, since 2007, lived partly in the Netherlands and partly in Hungary. About three weeks in the Netherlands and then two weeks in Hungary.

Since 2007 I also travelled a lot in Middle and Eastern Europe, most of the time with my son. During our travels I continued working. But that was easy because it was all in Europe. In 2018 we did the Trans Mongolia Express for three weeks. I was surprised that I could continue my work travelling through Russia, Mongolia and China as well. That was a real eye-opener to me. When my relationship broke up in October 2018 and we had to sell our house, I decided not to buy another house, but to start travelling. So I left the Netherlands in February 2019.

—Jan van Kuijk

After the breakdown of marriage, I was away from home a lot for work anyway, and there was no need to upset the living arrangements of anyone in the family home. I had actually separated from my marriage a few years before that, but we lived in the same house, under the same roof, until all four of our children finished high school. So it was a mutual decision. I'd come home weekends or sometimes not come home for a couple of weeks. And when I thought about it – about moving out and maybe getting my own place or something like that when the kids finish school – I worked out how much time I'd actually be in that home and it was only four weeks of a whole year. And I thought, "What a waste of money."

And so I literally launched into my community and they caught me and it was just fabulous. I didn't feel a fear. I'd also spent two years before I left talking to my children about what mum's life was going to look like as this is what I might do. I was getting them comfortable with the idea that I would be coming to visit them rather than the other way around, which I actually love now. They're all adults and they've got their own homes so I get to visit them and I don't do the dishes, don't make my bed and I leave the toilet seat up, wet towels on the floor, and I leave, which is really lovely.

But, I mean, I didn't have kind of a fear or a hesitation. Some people have said that it was very brave and I can't connect with that. Maybe bravery is in the eye of the beholder – other people kind of see it as brave, whereas for me it kind of felt quite natural.

—**Dee Brooks**

 **TOP TIPS!**

- Embrace the magic of simply showing up – you cannot possibly know everything before you set out.
- Trust that, no matter what, there will always be help and kind folk along the way.
- Don't waste time and energy convincing others why you are doing this – choose your tribe!

Home sweet home

OF COURSE, THE VERY IDEA of "home sweet home" is ironic and is the double-edged sword! The glee is simultaneously the glaring challenge – that of being constantly on the move. Or, as my Nan would say, "on the hoof." The itinerant nature of living #LocationFree is the aspect you will naturally wish to master quite fast. Getting over the notion that it is not so much a holiday, but rather a whole new lifestyle choice you have embarked on.

So, how will you navigate the idea of feeling at "home"? Part of it is the delight of being able to decide how long you stay before moving on to the next place. That is different for everyone on this journey, of course, and you really have to find the rhythm that works best for you (and whomever you are living with). Some folk I have met seldom stay more than a month in one place; others prefer to stay for three months. No rules, no obligation – just do what works best for your work, heart and budget.

Settling in

I realise now that I had a little unspoken rule to help me make sense of this new lifestyle. I honestly didn't know it was even happening at the beginning of this journey, because it was never a conscious "rule" per se, but as I look back now I see it clearly at play every step of the way.

If I was working onsite for a client and being flown in for the work and leaving a couple of days later – usually two, three or maybe four nights – I considered that "travelling for work". The moment I knew I was going to spend than about eight to 10 days in any one place, I allowed it to feel more like "home" for me. This meant that I approached it with a different kind of energy and that enabled the feeling of short-term commitment to kick into gear for me.

About two years into my #LocationFree journey, one of the invaluable lessons I learned from my chiropractor was that changing beds all the time can wreak havoc on your body, especially your back. I had started feeling really sore, achy, and quite weak in my back and hips and was worried that some old physical injuries had come back to haunt me. I have had to actively manage a back injury from my twenties and had suffered two badly herniated discs in the past eight years that needed two intense years of rehab. As a result, looking after my back has always required conscious effort. But more about that in Lesson 7!

I even started to worry that I had something serious like cancer. After consulting with my chiropractor, he essentially told me that I needed to build core strength. And so I became more careful about where I would stay for long periods of time. Having started this lifestyle in my late forties and being accustomed to relative comfort, I was definitely not about to start backpacking or living in shabby hostels with dodgy mattresses. Thanks to awesome clients, my busy work and travel schedule had afforded me the luxury of being able to stay in the best resorts or hotels money could buy and

I needed a way to cleverly emulate a version of "home" for myself. I had to feel my way into what was best for me and my body, mind and soul.

When I was put up in hotels for client functions and conferences, I would often stay longer by booking in earlier and extending my stay by paying the excess on the tab. That way I could "rest, relax and nest" in one bed, room, suite or apartment for eight to 10 days. Although to the outside world I was itinerant and constantly on the go, I had my own games to ensure that it somehow worked for me. I also learned to trust and use Airbnb. In six years I have only ever had one truly awful experience. That was in New York, and I was too exhausted to leave and book into a hotel for two nights. A more recent blip happened in Malaga, but the landlady was a rock star and between us we managed to sort it all out amicably. I still moved though, because the apartment was so noisy that I would never be able to settle in and I had prepaid for six weeks!

I thus adopt habits and rituals that support me – do you do that in your own way? Whether I am staying one night or two weeks, or even longer, I have some rituals I use to help me settle in.

Hello, home!

One of my ingrained travelling habits when I get to a new place is to throw open all the windows to let fresh air gush in. Just for 10 minutes if it's cooler weather! It rattles me a little to stay in hotel rooms that don't have windows that open! If the windows don't open I stand and take in the view while doing some deep intentional breathing. That instantly lifts me up one level. Then I text whoever I need to let them know that I arrived safely – my partner, my mum or the client. Next I unpack whatever is appropriate for that stay. This is followed by a shower (or long soaking bath if just off an international flight) and a cup of tea or coffee, depending on the time of day. Or wine, if it's early evening! Next I create my "working desk" so that all my tech and work stuff is where I need it to be, which settles me another layer in my "home."

Such simple things, but they keep me grounded and help me to know exactly what to do, step by step.

Neighbourhood jaunt

My next settling-in hack is one of my most important rituals. Something heart based and spiritual that allows me to connect super quickly to the physicality of a new place. For me, that is to find the *one* local coffee shop that I know I will adore, one that is also quite close by. I look for the one where the locals hang out, that is somewhat quirky, or typical of the area. The place I will then be able to consider my "local" for the duration of my stay.

I believe that if I can get to know every inch of one small square mile around where I am "living", I have successfully simulated and created a home base for myself. It also means that the second time I head to that same little coffee shop, I can say hello and know that they have seen me before, so it's also a way of being witnessed and seen along the journey. I can look for a friendly face to say hi to. And, if I know the language, I can even strike up more of a conversation to connect a layer deeper.

With the coffee shop pinpointed, I set out to find the closest grocery store with the longest hours and make that my local shop! It's amazing how, after two visits, if you smile and make eye contact, people come to recognise you! It doesn't take much to stand out when you make someone else matter! No matter how weak your command of the local language, an attempt at "Hello, how are you?" is always appreciated – and remembered! It's all about making effort. Travelling is about connecting and immersing yourself in the country you find yourself in. In my experience, staff will be far more helpful when they too are being seen, noticed and thanked for their work and effort. Kindness and acknowledgement go a long way for us as humans and, after all these years, I have found this to be my most valuable travelling and "settling in" wisdom.

Walk your way

My third ritual is to go for a much longer walk. To immerse myself, I simply walk and walk and walk some more. A good pair of trainers, a light shawl or jacket just in case, some water and a well-charged phone, that's all I need to explore. To experience, see, say hello, imbibe and witness. It helps me to feel as if I know the broader area a little more intimately. I sometimes keep a gentle eye on Google maps for orientation (maps.me is an even better app that works without any data or internet connection – priceless for travelling). At the end of this longer walk, depending on my energy levels and the distance covered, I might still walk home, or hop in a taxi cab or uber to get back to my new home with speed and ease.

On the flip side, though, if I am booked into a hotel for only a few days, travelling for big client work, I might not work my way through all of the above steps. After opening windows, unpacking, a shower and coffee, I might choose to stay within the confines of the hotel premises. This keeps me more focused until my work commitment is over and my mind can rest easy. It's only once my work obligations are fulfilled that I then set off on my adventures to explore before heading off on the next plane. In this scenario I will pick either the smallest coffee shop in the hotel, or the one closest to the pool with a fabulous view to consider my "local" and be sure to visit that same one during my stay. I will also choose one table for meals – usually because the same staff will serve that same table, so I achieve yet another layer of connecting.

Housesitting

When I was considering moving permanently to the USA, I just wanted to go and hang out there for longer stretches of time, to see how I liked it. You always have to engage with the legalities of working in your chosen country, so I was still working with clients online and earning money and paying taxes back in South Africa, and just living and travelling elsewhere. My passport and visa allow me to travel to the USA for up to 90 days at a time – so I did that a few times!

Finally, once I got tired of hotels and Airbnb apartments, I considered housesitting. The first time the idea dawned on me was at San Francisco airport. Faced with a three-hour delay and armed with a glass of Californian Sauvignon Blanc, I wondered how I would be able to revisit and still feel as though I was living there – to "try on" the city, so to speak, without making major commitments just yet. As far as modern cities go, San Francisco is notoriously expensive, so I needed to be super creative. Having de-cluttered the homes of hundreds of clients for more than a decade, I always find it exceptionally easy to make someone's place feel like home. It's been in my blood ever since I was a child. It just comes easy to me to make myself at home and ensure that people feel better when I leave. Whether I have been paid to do work in their home and de-clutter or organise, or, visiting a friend, I always try to ensure that they want me back. Well ... most people!

Sitting in the airport bar at San Francisco International, doing a bit of brainstorming and research, I stumbled upon an amazing housesitting website and soon after was also introduced to friends of a friend who had recently started doing the very same thing. Please see the resources in Lesson 10 for this great organisation. I realised that if I was staying in San Francisco that day I could have looked after two gorgeous Persian kittens in a four-storey duplex in Telegraph Hill, my favourite neighbourhood. That really got me thinking and my creative juices flowing!

You pay a small annual membership fee, need to be vetted and also submit references, for instance. The homeowners also pay a membership fee. Over the years, I had done relief management work for businesses, and been paid to look after umpteen homes, but mostly for people who knew and trusted me. But this was about finding a creative way to be in other countries and to immerse myself in the most expensive city in the USA. Thanks, Silicon Valley – maybe this was one way to do it!

Now … *Why* would I do this? This chapter is titled "Home sweet home", isn't it? And housesitting is precisely the opposite – it is *not* home. Others may look from the outside and think, Aaaah, it's because she doesn't want to pay to stay in hotels. But, nope, it was not that at all.

For me, it's all about *feeling at home*. Housesitting is not so much about the homes, but about the *animals*! Many people prefer to have someone to love their furry friends in their own home, rather than suffer the stress of placing them in kennels. And that afforded me a much-needed dose of four-paw love and a way of immersing myself in a residential community, mimicking living in that neighbourhood. Priceless. And, on my next visit to San Francisco, I got to house-/animal-sit five different homes in different areas that gave me a real experience of what living there might be like.

Housesitting is also a way to feel part of a community, as opposed to being just one of many strangers booked into the same hotel. The neighbours are locals, living a regular life around you. Usually, home owners bend over backward to make you feel at home: they let friends and neighbours know you are there, they leave numbers to call should something go wrong, and most often the use of a car or a bicycle comes with the territory. Often they recommend their favourite restaurants and bars, coffee shops and local spots a tourist would never find on their own. It's a way to fast track settling in and feeling at home, even if temporarily. To have a set of house keys, trash to put out, and post to bring in rather than carrying a hotel keycard to gain room access and deciding whether to put up the "Do Not Disturb" sign.

One of the hardest aspects of living #LocationFree and having no permanent home base has been dealing with the "loss" of Stripey, my cat – even though I can still visit and love him when I'm in Johannesburg. Living #LocationFree is not simply moving to another country where you can take your pets. It's a little hard to do that when moving internationally every few months. Of course, if you stay within one larger geographic area, such as the USA or Europe, it might be much easier to keep your pets with you. You have read about Nancy Benn who manages to travel with hers within Europe! I, on the other hand, had to manage my guilt, figure out how to cope with my longing for animal companionship and missing my partner's dogs when I was not at his South African home. It is also why I love to visit the same Greek village every year. I try to rent the same flat for summer that has my "pretend" Greek cat, Nikos. He allows me to call him "mine" for three to four months a year. It takes him a few days to dare speak to me again, but when he does, we are inseparable and he sleeps on my bed – much to the amazement of my landlady! But, of course, it breaks my heart when I have to leave again.

One of the very real costs of living #LocationFree is the number of hellos and goodbyes that constantly rattle through your ecosystem. Again, it's one of those double-edged swords that you have to manage and prepare for. Some days are easier than others, to be honest.

Another way to integrate into a residential community is to book an Airbnb, where you rent a private room in someone's home. That way you have onsite, local companionship. I have done that effectively a number times, depending on the circumstances. When in town for a conference, I often prefer to stay with others in an Airbnb home, because it's really a great way to connect with locals fast. However, if my workload requires me to do a lot of online coaching and mentorship, I definitely prefer the privacy of an entire Airbnb apartment to myself. Layered on top of that, I also found that if I was going through one of my lonely patches (because, yes, that does happen, folks), I prefer the company of others so I don't isolate myself too much. Whereas if I am feeling stronger and resilient, I might choose the privacy option and trust that I will still be inclined to get out, socialise, connect on meet-ups or start a writing group, for example. So it is about managing workload with privacy requirements alongside my emotional needs to find the balance between the two. No set rules.

Local living

Learn to think like a local by taking a tour of your city with a local guide, specifically someone who has lived in the area for years or has a particular interest in one of your hobbies. If you love music, that may mean visiting the local bars and folk clubs. If you love dancing, maybe it's all the salsa hot spots and dance classes. An author? Then go on a literary tour. Coffee your tipple? Go on a barista and roastery tour. Airbnb now has an entire "experience" section over and above the accommodation aspect. Get the insider's guide to where you are, so that you can walk around with a sense of belonging. Learn about a treasured bakery, the best beaches and the local markets to shop for fruits and vegetables. Discover the gems that aren't shared in any tour guide or on any map. In bigger cities, you might also opt to use the international "Hop-on hop-off" buses, for a fast-track perspective of a wide area.

There are so many great ways to tap into the local attractions a city offers, to shift from feeling like a tourist to living like a local in your head and heart. I do this as soon as possible after arriving in a new place. If the city I am in is easy to navigate on foot, I much prefer to join a walking tour with an independent local. Visit your local tourist info centre if Google doesn't work for you. Or, when in that first neighbourhood coffee shop, ask the locals!

I also strongly believe in buying as much local produce and goods as possible. Where possible, I bypass the chain stores and prefer to spend my money at smaller, personal, family-run shops, restaurants or boutiques.

Volunteer

If you are staying in one place for a few months, another way to settle in and connect is to immerse in the community by doing volunteer work. Take your pick of homeless shelters, animal rescue centres, beach clean-ups – whatever makes you feel useful. Offer your time and expertise to a local cause, especially if you are away from your loved ones and family over festive times, important holidays and birthdays, for instance. Those times of year can be especially lonely and giving back is a wonderful way to tide you over those times. If you can be of service, you will be more connected to humanity and more likely to appreciate where you are, to revel in the space you are currently calling home sweet home. I have spent many holidays on my own, and rather than falling into a potential pit of self-pity, being useful has proven to be the perfect antidote. It may even help you more than it does the recipient of your time!

To illustrate, I was once in Malaga for four months over the winter and was on my own for Christmas. With no family in the country and having split up with my partner just a few days previously, it was a potentially dreadfully lonely time. I knew I had to do something purposeful and proactive so as to not feel sorry for myself. I tried to offer my time to a local charity shelter, but they were not taking any more volunteers, unless they were fluent in Spanish. Uh-oh ... Although I was having Spanish lessons I was by no means fluent. But I was tired of crying following my break-up and needed to do *something*, so I came up with a plan of my own. I bought festive boxed truffle chocolates and doggie treats. On Christmas morning I called my mum for her birthday (yes, on Christmas Day) and then cycled into the city centre, playing my own version of Mother Christmas.

Having already been in the city for eight weeks, I knew where most of the homeless folk hung out in their special spots, so I went looking for them armed with human and doggie treats. I knew they were all being fed a main meal by the shelter, so my aim was to offer a little treat. So I spent the morning delivering and patting doggies and it brought me so much joy to share some sweet love with them. Then I managed to grab a late lunch outdoors with two friends I had met at co-working meet-ups. That Christmas has become one of my all-time favourite memories.

 **WHAT OTHERS SAY ABOUT ...**

Home sweet home

A long time ago I made the shift to stop defining home as where I am physically and start defining it as where I am spiritually. So in that sense I always feel grounded no matter where I am, as long as I just maintain that internal connection. However, because I do travel around, I also do find myself creating community. I tend to love to host events and so a lot of times I will go to the Digital Nomad Facebook groups before I get to a country. I start talking with people and I will sometimes even throw events in those locations, just events for people to get to know each other. So a lot of times I find myself creating opportunities for people to meet and then, through that, meeting a lot of people myself.

In terms of accommodation, I tend to book an Airbnb for about a week and that will give me some time to really feel out a new location. From there I will find something more longer term, depending on how I feel about the place where I am.

—Gene Ellis

The most crucial thing I have found is to stick to your routine and bring a few precious mementoes with you. While travelling and having pictures of your excursions or places visited, your heart yearns for those reminders of what is home to you – mine are a few pictures of my girls and granddaughter, a few pashminas, which I pack to use not only as a fashion accessory, but I always have small hooks in my room that I hang them on to act as a wall hanging. My Bible and a 365-day daily devotional are also part of my arsenal to keep me grounded. I have never stopped my routine of waking up at 5.20 am, getting dressed and going for a walk for an hour first thing every day. This is my quiet time, reflection and gratitude time, and I use this habit to not only get the blood flowing and metabolism jumpstarted, but set my intentions for the day.

Another non-negotiable is my collapsible kettle [see the resources in Lesson 10]. The amount of times I've not been able to make a cup of coffee has made this a non-negotiable. If, like me, you're adventurous with food and drinks, it's wonderful to be able to brew your new country's coffee. But also vital to have a good cuppa of your faithful at hand if you find yourself missing home.

Lastly, commit to connecting with your loved ones back home. Life gets busy. Often, while you are experiencing new things and places, the routine of life back home remains and people carry on, without you being in their space. The hardest reality is that there are times when there is no one available to share your joy, either from a great workshop delivered, or a sight where you are enjoying a celebratory drink, and then wish to share the moment with your people back home, but they are not on the same timeline as you. Don't take this personally – although you will in the beginning. Life ebbs and flows, and sometimes we connect, and sometimes this moment is meant ... just for you. No blame, no guilt, just a fact. Lastly, square your shoulders and get out there and meet new people. I was encouraged to make a friend in each department on board the ship. I could kiss my daughter every day for that nugget of advice! Your new community doesn't yet know what they have in you if you don't show up and show them. This is something we really need to own. Put yourself in situations, share your expertise, kindness, compassion and drive so you can be witnessed and utilised by your new community. It will surprise you how soon you become part of a new fabric that is being woven. You need it just as much as the new surrounding needs you, trust me.

—**Deborah Louise Botha**

Most of our homes have been booked through Airbnb or similar so I became adept at scrutinising the listing and photos, looking for the amenities and searching the area on Google Maps and Street View, quite often finding the exact location. I'd research the area before we arrived and then quiz the host for insider information on where to go and what to see. Hosts are usually very flattered when we praise the beauty of their country and local area so are eager to share their knowledge.

I use the internet to find out more about the local community, searching the local council website and tourist information for events and highlights, even looking on Facebook for any community groups. Google Maps is invaluable for finding local supermarkets and services, and identifying emergency services, the local health centre and vets, etcetera.

Upon arriving in a new location, we head for the nearest bar and, if there are English-speaking customers, engage in conversation, sharing our experiences and asking for their views on the locality. We love to take the opportunity to attend any events and festivals too and have, quite by accident, been present for some great experiences.

I'm organised at packing and have our own covers to protect the sofas from dog hair so, with those in place, the home soon begins to feel like ours. However, I do love moving into a new place, settling in to a different environment and exploring the area.

I also move the furniture around to suit our needs, taking photos if necessary to ensure we know how to replace everything when we leave. I need a place to work from, so my priority is to identify a suitable table and room, or quiet corner, usually facing out of the window.

—Nancy Benn

Paul Young said it best: "Wherever I lay my hat, that's my home." And so I rearrange! Almost always. I de-clutter the new space of things like excess cushions on the bed (this happens everywhere except at my actual home in South Africa, where my partner loves the bloody cushions :-) and find an unused corner to tuck the TV away if it takes up space. I pack away things on the kitchen counter that I won't use.

I always make sure I have a desk and chair and I usually rearrange the room so that the desk is closest to the natural light and the window.

I strongly advise unpacking immediately. I find a place for all my creature comforts. My Bialetti coffee pot goes on the stove, my Bose bluetooth speaker finds a place to plug in and play and it is turned on almost immediately. I find a local radio station to listen to whilst unpacking.

Wherever possible, I put picked flowers or greenery into a vase or glass. I get my bathroom goods in place. Once organised, I shower and rest.

The first thing I usually do after that is to go for a long walk and try to orientate myself. I dine solo at a local restaurant and, when there is an opportunity, I chat to the staff. I find out their names and return to the same place a few times. I find that this is a great way to get local advice and to feel comfortable and at home in a new location.

—Lynne Scullard

Most of the places we've lived since leaving Canada we've sought out the art community and we start creating art. If there is a tattoo shop nearby, I usually have a chat with the owner.

If we don't have a painting job lined up, we look for a house to rent and in developing nations the rent is quite reasonable. We also travel slowly, staying in one place for up to three months. This helps us stay grounded.

The accommodation varies from location to location. Before we made our way out of Canada, we accepted the fact that we probably would be staying in places that are not on par with Canadian building-code standards.

We've lived in places ranging from wonderful beach houses with all the amenities, to jungle houses that are open to nature, and to adobe houses on the edge of the desert.

—Chris de Cap

I spend as much time as possible meeting new people but also keeping my own rituals. Small things like meditation, walking in nature, and appreciation bring me back to the moment and I feel like I'm home. The rule I use is "be curious" with people, culture and places. Read as much as you can about the location you're in, talk to locals about good spots and secret places. I tend to have one or two cafés I always go to where the baristas say hi so I make that my home. I take one day "off" from people to ground myself and tidy up my place. It brings a little bit of structure to the chaos of living in a new place. I sometimes have the tendency to hermit and focus a little too much on my work so I leave the house every day, even if it's a walk around the block.

—Carolynne Alexander

When I was moving from place to place, I would look up Facebook groups for Digital Nomads in that country, city, or island. Co-working spaces are excellent for making new friends and settling into a new community. In bigger Digital Nomad hubs like Chiang Mai you can sign up for workshops or classes that offer another opportunity to mingle with like-minded folk.

As for accommodation, I'd always get an apartment or guesthouse room for a week, which gave me enough time to check out longer-term accommodation. By saying "I don't smoke" and "I don't party" (if applicable) or offering to pay various months up front, you can try to knock some more off the rental price.

—André Gussekloo

When I travel on my own, it's still challenging finding community and feeling at home. That feels more like travel, but when I'm travelling with the Unsettled group, having an apartment with housemates, that feels more like living.

—Uday Jhunjhunwala

I have stayed in so many Airbnbs and I am really particular about picking places that look and feel homely. It doesn't take me long to settle into a new place as long as I have my essentials, good wifi, candles (they make me feel grounded), some books, comfortable bedding and a well-stocked kitchen.

In terms of settling into a new community, for me this comes from researching and looking into local events and meet-ups. When I first came to Malaga I found a great co-working event, which helped me to settle in quickly and make new friends and connections. I feel like living in this way you have to really put yourself out there and seek out the people and places that will help you to feel part of the local community.

—Victoria Jane Watson

During my sabbatical, instead of the planned round-the-world "tourist" trip, I spent a lot of time living and travelling as a volunteer, going from place to place. So I stayed in dormitories or other shared accommodation with fellow volunteers. I never really gave it much thought that I didn't have my own private space most of the time; wherever I put my backpack, I was home. For me "being home" is about being happy, not about being in a particular place. I just settle in, period. Maybe my trick is not to have goals/wants/needs, but just to accept my surroundings as is, and go from there. Or move on if it doesn't suit or match with me for whatever reason.

As an example of accepting the surrounds as is, in the case of housesitting, I accept the care structure that is offered to me by the home owners (feeding, grooming and walking and sometimes medicating animals, etcetera) almost literally, and then during my stay it slowly turns into my own thing, while keeping in line with the instructions of the home owners of course.

—**Martin van den Berg**

I ground myself through walking barefoot on the edge of the water on a beach or sitting or being in nature. Feeling at home is inside my body. Sometimes I say that home is when I know where my favourite coffee mug is – early mornings with coffee and writing are my favourite.

—**Mette Glargaard**

I'm a big fan of Facebook groups: that's the fastest way to get your social circles going. I already start making contacts before moving and when we get to a new location, I start meeting with people immediately. I also create groups of like-minded people or create a lot of events and meet-ups in existing groups just to meet more people. I believe that the more you make contacts, the sooner you find "your kind of people". My interests are very versatile, so it's very easy for me to say "yes" to different kinds of activities and events. To feel at home, I need people I can call friends. When I was young, I moved with very little things. Now, when moving to a new place, it's a lot of suitcases, but then again, we are not travelling, we move more to live in that place. We get a rental apartment, usually from the local rental market, but sometimes through Airbnb, and I decorate it with items and textiles we have brought with us to create a feeling of home. I'm a huge fan of Ikea, because there I always find inexpensive stuff that pleases my eye and makes a more homely feeling. We also try to find apartments that are furnished in the "Ikea style".

—**Katia Enbuske**

I'm blessed that my attitude in life is like Paul Young sang in his song "Wherever I Lay My Hat That's My Home". My laptop and internet connection are my connection to the world, my family, my friends and my customers. For me, it was necessary for the first time in October to settle myself into Malaga. The co-working space and Kate's writing group helped a lot!

—**Jan van Kuijk**

I believe that this particular lifestyle is going to become more and more popular and so more and more products will come onto the market. I'm happy to tell you that I'm a big Airbnb user, but there may be another product that comes onto the market that's similar or better to Airbnb. But I use it almost all of the time. I'm going to Patagonia next month and I've Airbnb-ed my accommodation. I have criteria that are important to me and I plug in that criteria and see what comes up.

Please do not hesitate to negotiate for longer rates. What I do, my hack, is that I spot the apartment I want to stay in, then I contact the host before I book or reserve because Airbnb used to allow a pause between "I'd like to reserve this place" and "Okay, you need to pay now". Now you immediately pay. So I try to pause that process by contacting the host with a bunch of queries. "Hi, is your wifi really good because I need to work?" and "Hi, I'm staying for X number of days, would you consider a discount?" And most landlords do – they're quite comfortable with a discount and they'll send you an offer to say, "Yes, here's your 5%."

I did once go outside the Airbnb platform – I Airbnb-ed it for several years here in Santiago when I first arrived, all over the city, and with one of the landlords I did negotiate a longer-term deal outside of that platform. We linked it up to my PayPal account so she'd just send me a PayPal request and I'd put the rent through. It is risky, though, because with that landlord and I, our relationship ended because winter came, the electricity went up because of heating of the apartment, and she freaked out and said, "You've got to pay more." And then I wanted the protection of Airbnb because she was pushing me to negotiate outside the site. So I eventually terminated that deal and moved on somewhere else.

I wonder if I'm a grounding-into-a-new-space kind of person? I do have a process or a ritual. It's get into the place, check out what's there, what's not, empty my backpack so I can go shopping because no one gets plastic bags anywhere. I use my apps on my phone, of which I've got several, to direct me to the nearest supermarket. I have simplified my life in terms of what I buy in a supermarket, how I cook and what I eat. So now I've pretty much got a standard sort of shopping list so that I don't make my life too complicated. Of course, I want to try whatever's local and yummy. I bring that back, ensure that my wifi works, get all settled up and then start to plan my days when am I going to work, when am I going to photograph.

It depends if I need to get involved with the community or not. Obviously, in Santiago I needed to get involved with the community because this was more of a permanent base. So first, I look into my own community. I'm a coach so I look into the coaching community. I'm always welcome there. And I follow my various hobbies, the photography community, the yoga community, the women's groups. I volunteer very often in leadership positions so that I am able to have some important conversations.

I niche myself in English. I do that purposefully despite many people's suggestion that I should learn Spanish and immerse myself in the Spanish-speaking community. But once I do that I'm competing with thousands of other Spanish coaches who know exactly what they're doing and have mastery. So I know what I'm doing and have mastery in English and so I niche into that marketplace. So the expat communities, inter-nations and meet-up groups are my go-to places.

—**Michelle Clarke**

My community is digital – my main form of travel is for work, so, if I have a few spare days, I put my hand up to my communities online and ask who wants me – Halifax, Chicago or Dublin.

Now I've got the tingles. I had an incident happen. Well, it's probably not an incident. It was probably very intentional of the universe. It was very early on, in my first year, and I was doing some work in Indonesia. As I said before, I talked to my children, we knew this is what mum's going to do, it was all organised. It was fine and I just had this moment. I was walking down this really busy street in Indonesia and this big jolt, almost kind of like a panic attack, but I went, "Huh, I've got no home!"

And so I stopped right there in the middle of this busy street and I shut my eyes and I grounded myself to the earth. I just went into this meditation and I found the true meaning of the saying "Home is where your heart is". I just had this moment when I started crying in the street and everyone's looking and saying, "What's wrong with the white lady?"

It really hit home and I just felt it so profoundly. And I've never felt that ever, ever again. And then another thing happened that same trip – it must have been playing on my mind a bit – but I felt it. I felt, no, this is where home is, wherever I am is home. And I had a dream: I was in a hotel in Surabaya in Indonesia and I woke up from this dream and this quote was ringing through my head. I don't know who was saying it in my dream or if it was me. I don't know what it was. But the quote was, "She never felt like she fit anywhere so instead she decided to fit everywhere." And I wrote that down.

I like hotels for their sparseness but also like being in someone's home for the homeliness – I get itchy feet after about three weeks.

When I'm going over to the UK – so when we're going towards time, not back in time from Down Under – I can land over there and go straight to work. I feel like I can be very prepared. When I come back east, the jetlag hits harder so I know not to book anything in for those couple of days. With the practical aspects of the actual preparation for that travel, it's usually more through conversations and I talk to the people who are co-hosting with me or who are hosting the space or delivery. I need to get into the space that we're going to be working in and walk the space. It's almost a kind of meditative walk in that I can visualise people in there and movements and what's going to happen.

For myself, what I like to do when I first wake up in the morning is I like to meditate for at least – and it's not long – 15 or 20 minutes. If I can't do that I will still make sure I have at least one minute of quiet mindfulness ... It's something that I do that is just for myself and to prepare myself for the day. And that's work or not work – I like to have just some kind of small part of time. I've taken to setting my alarm half an hour earlier than I used to, giving myself a bit more spaciousness so I can take that time. I can't remember the last time I did just a one-minute meditation because I try to make sure I have that bit of space. Yeah, I think that's more about getting the sense and *the feeling of the space that I'm in and being prepared to really warmly welcome people.*

—Dee Brooks

 **TOP TIPS!**

- Make peace with juggling the exhilaration of freedom and adventure with missing a permanent home base.
- Remember, you chose this so you can make new decisions at any time.
- Be bold about curating this lifestyle – seek out your sweet spot to call "home".

Doing business #LocationFree

UNLESS YOU ARE ALREADY A true digital/tech worker and pretty well versed in working remotely or online, you might find the most important shuffle when it comes to doing business #LocationFree happens in your head. Believing in the new ideas and thoughts around what is possible. Any and every possible permutation of this lifestyle is yours for the choosing. Really! All the stories shared here should show you that no matter your age, country of origin, desired destination, work experience – CEO, virtual assistant, artist, coach, brand specialist or pet-sitter – it *is* 100% possible.

You simply have to believe that you are able to create your own version that works for *you*. Be inspired by the ideas of others but, more importantly, have the courage to find the most relevant way forward for you and your specific business model. Test your ideas and theories. Try it for a short time or, like me, set a predetermined cut-off date. I initially thought I was going to live this way for a year – that felt exciting, tangible and completely doable to me. Extending the adventure felt natural when, about nine months into the first year, I knew that I would not be ready to stop within the 12-month period. And here I am, five years in, knowing that the sixth year is unfolding in the same exhilarating way.

You might need to try it on and do some live testing out in the world. Push the boundaries with your clients or bosses to see whether anyone protests. Or did you perhaps *expect* them to protest and, because that is your own preconceived idea, you've blocked yourself from trying it out? What I do know for sure is that you *are* ready and just need that final nudge from the nest.

Of course, if anyone does bleat too loudly, it might be time to make a decision about who you work for and how you work … You don't have to *jump* in unless you are ready to. Everyone can take incremental steps; try some remote living or co-working to see how you manage in the trenches.

You're craving adventure, freedom and passion? How far do you need to push your boundaries?

Your business and working arrangements are dependent only on what you can conjure up for yourself. I started this book talking about mindset, because I believe that that is the most significant factor in deciding whether you can or will live #LocationFree.

Of course, recent world events have meant that many more of us now realise that working away from the office and more remotely is indeed possible – imagine that! I firmly believe that this will allow more and more people to be drawn to the possibility of not being glued to a single location for work. Of course, you can still *choose* to be in one location, but perhaps it is making the possibility of gallivanting a little easier for you? Being forced into it means that leaders, managers, employees and business owners are fast accepting that things are shifting. While this terrifies most, it is also the key to realising that the freedom of a different lifestyle is much closer than you ever dreamed possible.

The very first thing you need to own in your heart and mind is that it is possible to run a successful business and work from wherever your choose. Of course, we all have certain criteria that are important to our choices, but those are yours to design and implement in your ideal life.

Conceiving it in your heart, and dreaming about it, is the most important trigger – the flame that will ignite your dream. Up until now, you may only have heard about someone else (like me) doing it, or perhaps you read an article, or dreamed about travelling and working abroad since you were a child. Naturally, I am not referring to millionaires, retirees or anyone with a golden goose nest egg who are not required to work. I am also not referring to students and millennials backpacking around the world on a gap year. Nor am I referring to folk basically wanting to run away from life and their responsibilities. I refer here to you and me – regular folk, with our feet on the ground (most of the time, anyway) and dreams as lofty as sea birds. People with real businesses to run, or jobs we are responsible for that are about serving clients and earning money. Using travel, freedom and choice as anchors in life.

You can be single, married, divorced or anything in between, because the thread that binds #LocationFree workers together is simply wanting some semblance of freedom from the regular nine-to-five, not being tied to one place, not clocking in to a job, not necessarily pocketing the safety net of a regular salary. Yes, there are folk who work remotely for companies with a more fixed and secure regular income and that is another fantastic way to design your own life: you have the security of being part of a company, with the freedom of not having to commute.

Remote working is fast becoming more of a norm, especially in light of what happened during lockdown following the outbreak of the

Covid19 world pandemic; it saves time, money, commuting and, of course, reduces emissions into the atmosphere by limiting traffic on the roads, lessens our carbon footprint. As long as companies have sound digital platforms, secure accessibility and a forward-thinking leader and frame of mind for the work model, this way of working offers security alongside flexibility to spend more time (or some of the time) at home, more quality time with the family, and a better overall lifestyle. I believe working remotely is going to become far more mainstream in the near future.

In general, when I refer to a #LocationFree lifestyle, I refer to individuals who are usually self employed, run their own companies, freelance or are contracted and are more in charge of their commitments than those of us who are tied into one physical location or employer. At the end of the day, however, none of these distinctions really matters; neither does what you call it. As you read earlier, people think of this and refer to this lifestyle in different ways.

The model of #LocationFree living and working generally centres around the following:
- Freedom
- Inspired possibility
- Flexibility
- Choices and consequences
- Vital and engaged living
- Passion and purpose
- Courageous living
- Travelling and exploring
- Exposing yourself to new places, cultures, food, customs and lifestyles.

The #LocationFree mindset is about being able to travel the world, seeing and experiencing people, cultures and places, while simultaneously having the flexibility to work along the way, and earn your living, no matter what.

In this day and age, with the advent of technology and the accessibility of travel, it is becoming easier and easier, from a practical point of view, to implement it and the greatest obstacle is often the internal *mindset*.

Let's start with the business mindset … To run a #LocationFree business, you will need to have five main attributes in bucket loads:

1. Courage

As with any entrepreneur, solo-preneur or freelancer, courage goes without saying. But when you are considering travelling the world and working, your courage needs to be amped up a notch. You cannot know all the ins and outs from the get go. If you are risk averse, you will never leave the comfort of your job or home. If you need to know every map of every city before you get there, where is the fun in exploring? Or perhaps it just takes you longer to plan and you need more money as a safety net before you can set off on your adventurous life? I have found that courage must be at the top of your list to make life appealing and successful – carving it into something that fulfils rather than terrifies you. Living and working #LocationFree is not something you can embark on just because you feel other people need you to, or expect you to, or because you feel you have to prove it to yourself. You will be miserable and depressed in no time at all. This needs to be a deep calling, a yearning from within, and a willingness to let go of the shore and let the boat float on the open seas and explore new lands. It requires a sense of adventure along with the courage. And you will have to remind yourself of this time and time again, or be part of a community who reminds you when you forget.

I remember the first time I learned about "values" and how to establish what mine were. I whittled them down from about 20, distilling my list to three single values that drive me no matter what. My top one is courage, followed by freedom and then honesty. So, if ever I found myself feeling like a "poor little thing" throwing myself a pity party, I would remind myself of this important value and find the courage of the Bengal tiger to dig deep and just jump.

I also play the game of trying to consider what is the very worst that can ever happen if it all went belly up and pear-shaped? What could I lose, what trouble might I get into? What might be the absolute worst-case scenario? If I can make peace with that, then I can usually find a way forward, because at that point I am no longer controlled by the fear of it all. I have shone a light on the possible screw-ups, can put some measure into place in order to reduce the fall-out or mitigate the risk, and so the worst typically never happens. But it is the fear of the worst happening that will debilitate us.

2. Resilience

"Resilience" is quite the buzzword nowadays, one that refers – in my mind – to your "bounce-ability." How are you able to feel things deeply in order to process them, allow them to move through you as they unfold, and simultaneously not be derailed by them for too long? I'm definitely not advocating deferring or ignoring problems when they arise, or drinking or drugging them away in any form. Rather, I am suggesting that it's about being able to get back up on that flying horse sooner rather than later.

How? I have two games that I play – try them!

The first is the "5.5 wail" and the second the lesser-spotted "24-hour wallow." Each is called upon at different times for different reasons.

The "5.5 wail" is required when I am in the middle of a tight deadline, have lots on my plate and am thus experiencing heightened stress levels. You know … when you need a few more cups of coffee than usual? I might suddenly hit a wall, or something triggers me deeply and I tumble into an emotional hole. And – *Bam!* – it's all suddenly too much.

It is at that point that I give myself a "5.5 wail" time-out. I set the clock and let myself cry, scream or wail for five and a half minutes. I might even write the word F^%$ over and over again for the full 5.5 minutes. It's very therapeutic! But when my alarm goes off, that's it, Kate – get up, wipe the tears, go to the bathroom, pour yourself some coffee/water/wine and just get back to it. Stop the pity party after 5.5 minutes.

Why 5.5? Because that's enough time to let you feel it all without slipping too far down the hole and thus allowing the wail to become the wallow when it really doesn't need to. Sometimes wails just need a bit of airtime.

I also love to employ the lesser-spotted "24-hour wallow" as and when required. I guess that's what you call a duvet day, when you simply stay home from work? Or the ones in the movies that involve empty bottles, pizza boxes, wine, tissues and dishes piled high until the trusted friend arrives, poking their head around at the door to save the day.

When I feel as though life is going south, I occasionally let myself off the hook by giving myself a little more leeway. A slightly deeper hole to fall down. And by this I mean not just regular time-out, recharge time or holidays built in into my year, I mean when I can feel a deep pity-party mood coming on. I might have just finished some long-haul travel after a tough work week, or am feeling lonely and exhausted and wondering what the hell I am doing and why am I not living like a "regular person". The self-doubt, self-berating WTF moment that punches me in the solar plexus. When that monster rears its ugly head, I allow myself to wallow for the entire day until 6 am the following morning. There are two tricks to this method of resilience – the alarm clock and sticky notes!

I grab the tissues and set my alarm for 6 am the next morning. Next I write two sticky notes with a very short list of what I will do the moment that alarm goes off at 6 am: *Get up, water, stretch, coffee, look fab, work!* It plays out like this as I follow the sticky note step by step:

- 6 am alarm – get up, Kate!
- Drink hot lemon water.
- Do stretching yoga for 20 minutes (don't push for too long and risk not actually getting down to it).
- Journal for 10 minutes over a cup of fresh coffee.
- Shower and dress to look fab – that means lipstick and even a pair of heels!
- Start work at 8 am sharp.

On my desk I have a second sticky note that simply reads: *mail 3, SM, friend* and *book it*:

- Fire up the computer and send three emails.
- Make one social media post (even if that means sharing my crap day).
- Call one friend for support.
- Book some self-care this week.

That self-care appointment may be a massage, getting my hair or nails done, some body work or energy healing, for example. Something to remind myself that I am important and that self-care is vital. I also remind myself that the latter is a deductible expense and part of running a business!

So there is one Post-it next to my bed and another on my laptop and I make myself a promise that when I wake up I just need to read the Post-it notes and follow each of them one by one. No-brainer. Step by step.

Once that's done, I can get down to wallowing and wailing and whining in my private pity party. Watch movies in my PJs, eat pizza, drink wine, cry, and punch a pillow. But I also know this self-indulgence has a cut-off point. The bottom line is that when I have given myself a "24-hour wallow" I can generally bounce back into my resilient zone and get on with working and living my life. (Disclaimer! It hasn't always worked, of course …)

Bigger curve balls hit every now and then, don't they? If I realise that a pity party is fast on its way to becoming a wallow fest, and looks to be settling in for more than 24 hours, I have to figure out a different way through. Sometimes it's simply a matter of digging deeper and deeper into the self-care and taking more drastic action. Or calling on friends or mentors for advice and an ear. (See more in Lesson 7 about becoming more resilient.)

3. Patience

All business ventures require patience. When you have stepped beyond the confines of what had once been your everyday life – your long-established routines and the stability of having a home, friends, family and job with a natural rhythm you have developed over the years – you are going to need far more patience to live a lifestyle that is vastly different to what you have experienced before and actually revel in it.

Clients and contracts often take a lot longer to "land". It might take more business "foreplay" in persuading a client to trust and work with you online. Or they might prefer to wait until you revisit your "home" country.

Travel delays, learning to getting around in new cities and settling in also require patience. I have found over the past five years that I usually need to factor in about one week of real settling-in time once I have landed in a new location. I don't mean when I'm zipping in and out for work or am in tourist mode, but rather when I get to a new spot where I'll be staying for a longer period. Despite all my settling-in rituals, I have come to work with that rhythm of allowing a one-week landing time. In that week, I allocate the work accordingly, and in this way am kinder and more patient with myself while I establish a new routine and acclimatise to the time zone and weather, for instance. There is no point getting pissed off, angry, judgemental and unkind to myself.

When you are working globally, you have to allow for time zones, climate, cultures and different ways in which things are done. That requires adjustments, making allowances and some degree of tolerance. Different countries have different weekends, celebration days or holidays (think Middle East, which has a Friday-and-Saturday weekend). It's all about patience and letting things be so that the events unfold in their own time. It is far less stressful to accept it than resist it because resistance simply eats up vital energy.

4. Trust

Trust is part of the mindset you need in order to ace your business and personal life. You cannot allow your mind to play tricks on you – and have to learn to rely on your gut. As a woman travelling alone most of the time, I need to know and intuit when my life is in danger, or when not to walk down an alley at night even when Google Maps is pointing me that way. We all need to have our wits about us wherever we are in the world, full stop.

But I believe that we need yet another layer of self-trust when living #LocationFree. How do you let yourself trust what country, what city and what area to choose? Where to book accommodation? The interplay between tapping into that energy of excitement and the unknown and, simultaneously, not second-guess yourself has to become second nature to you and your way of life.

I carry certain mantras within myself, but for the most part I work with "Just trust it". When there is even an inkling to go somewhere or to reach out, I try my best to follow through. Likewise, if I get a nagging feeling not do something, I don't try to talk myself into it. It almost always backfires when I ignore that little voice. No matter how much your thinking brain may try to override it, quieten your gut or tell you why you should and how it will work out or make you money, if you don't trust your gut and the decisions you have made, then you have essentially given your power away and put your trust in everyone else instead. That is not going to make you feel safe or self-reliant when travelling and spending a lot of time on your own.

5. Alone time

Living and working #LocationFree suggests that you might spend a lot of time on your own, so it's important that you come to terms with that early on in your adventure, particularly if that may interfere with, disrupt or detract from your ability on the work front. You may need to make tough business decisions on the go, without being able to check in with your usual business Masterminds, peers, mentors or consultants. Even when you have a fabulous team in place to support your business, you will – in my experience – also be faced with a lot of solo time and decision-making.

Do you like yourself in the quiet of the night, when there is no one else to talk to or check in with you? Are you truly okay sightseeing on your own, or striking up conversations with strangers? Are you cool hanging out with yourself? At the end of a long workday delivering workshops, or working online, can you go to the bar for a drink on your own? Do you actually like who you are and feel comfortable in your own skin? This is a skill that can be learned and gets easier with time. But if you are lonely or don't enjoy spending too much time on your own, then you might just have to plan accordingly to reduce time alone. You could perhaps choose co-living spaces or co-working environments with "hot" desks you can rent.

To help keep the loneliness or even self-isolation at bay, ensure friends or family visit at different intervals, revisit places you know, or travel with your partner or colleagues from work. Everyone has to find what works best for them, but I did find that in the absence of usual stability and comforts, you might have to apply a little more effort in this department. It can be very useful to build in Mastermind gatherings a few times a year to ensure you are getting that boost of like-minded peer support.

It's just too easy to exist within a bubble and rely on family, friends and your work network in your regular life. You know the rhythm of your city, where to take an important new client for drinks on Thursday night, what concerts and ball games happen throughout the year, and where to buy last-minute Halloween costumes for your kids when your presentation runs late, for example. Life just has a repetitive rhythm that can make us complacent about reaching out and making new friends and expanding our business contacts. There is a level of comfort in how we exist day to day, week to week, and year to year, and we may find ourselves flailing when all of that is snatched away when we are not "home" or working in familiar territory.

So, now that we have outlined the mindset you might have to cultivate to be successful living #LocationFree, let's get down to the nuts and bolts of how to run a business under circumstances that are out of the ordinary:

Legalities

First of all, you always have to be registered for tax somewhere in the world. You cannot *not* have an address – everyone needs a footprint somewhere. Where you reside and where your business is registered might in truth be different places, of course. I will never forget the time when someone said to me, "Aah, so you are homeless and you travel the world so you don't have to pay tax, eh?"

Um no! If you know anything about me at all, you'll know that one of my top values is honesty, and I have always been above board with tax and government regulations. For the past 25 years my business has been based in South Africa. I have been at different times a sole proprietor, director of a Pty Ltd company, been a member in a CC (South African entity), and am currently director of my own company The Quick Shift Deva, Pty Ltd. It is only recently, in 2020, that I switched all of this to be based in Europe.

South Africa is therefore no longer my official base for tax or my work residence. But up until then, all my business dealings were done through the South African Reserve Bank, and tax was paid in that country. All above board. You cannot exist in a vacuum, even when living #LocationFree.

Because of where you were born, what passport you carry, and the specific legal requirements and residential rules for your country, everyone's situation will be different and you will have to figure this out for yourself. It is best to get professional advice and consult with tax accountants, international tax accountants, lawyers and emigration specialists as required. The best way is to tap into your local network to find people you trust and respect. But, above all, no matter how you are living and working, your business needs to be registered somewhere legally and personally. This book is not about how to dodge the system in any form.

Expenses

One of the challenges I had to overcome was how to find a way to get my cash slips and invoices to my accountant in South Africa while flitting between as many as six countries a year and thus working in multiple currencies for travel and personal expenses. At one point, my accountant used Sage Accounting, which has an app to which you upload cash slips for claiming expenses. When I changed accountants I needed a new system. Now, in the 2020s, there are umpteen easy ways to do this. There are apps that are country specific where you and your accountant have access to documents online. I, however, can be a little old fashioned sometimes – even with all my forward thinking – because I also like things to be uber simple and easy for me when I'm on the move.

I have a virtual assistant based in South Africa; I email any invoice I send clients or receive from service providers, and she then prints and couriers them to my accountant – also in South Africa. At the end of every month, I send proof of expenses to my accountant via WhatsApp, detailing each of my expense claims; she then loads them into her accounting package. I have done this for the last four years and it's worked brilliantly.

I also have to detail the various currencies from different countries and she adjusts them accordingly as expenses into ZAR (South African rand). The bottom line, then, is: please get professional advice and stay above board so that this aspect of your business does not zap one ounce of negative energy from you, and all your affairs remain in order. Simple, yet professional.

I do all my own invoicing and always have. It keeps me in touch with my cash flow. Perhaps you have an accountant or an accounting package that does that for you?

Banking

At one point I was selling a lot of online courses through my own online shop, which was connected to a shopping cart that integrated into my ZAR bank account. South Africa is a very specific neck of the woods and what works for you in countries such as the USA, Canada or all of Europe might not be applicable to South Africa. I had to find a way for my online CMS (content management system), called Infusionsoft, to work with my Wordpress website, the locally based shopping cart, and integrate that all with my bank account. It took three months to figure all of that out. Nowadays a lot of people use PayPal as a way to invoice clients and you can integrate PayPal with your local bank account to access your funds, or use PayPal to purchase services and goods online.

There are also crypto cards, which are linked to your crypto currency. Or international banks, such as Transferwise, which I now use to invoice international clients in different currencies.

Let's also talk about access to money when travelling. Some destinations offer special travel wallet cards. Because I have been on the move for a long time, I have found that one of the best ways to handle different currencies and different banks is to always have three different cards and accounts that I can access. No matter what, every time I crossed the border of South Africa, I had to allocate up to 45 minutes to call the bank in order to log where I was travelling for the following three months so that they could unlock my cards for pre-approval. That way my card usage would not be tagged as fraudulent transactions. Nowadays, you can activate this feature using your online banking app – when it works, of course. I was once caught out by trying to activate the app from the airport and the system was down, so I couldn't log in or get it to work. By then it was too late to call the bank. Tricky trip that one, fielding international fraud departments!

Navigating banking transactions, the suspicion of fraud, different countries and a multitude of cards can be tricky, so I live by the principle of "Be prepared". My rule is to have multiple cards that have money available in them, which ensures I am always liquid in some form. I also always travel with some cash on me, just in case – the local currency of the place I'm passing through, as well as the main international currencies of dollars and euros. With some of those in your wallet you can usually get by until you are able to make other arrangements for cash.

The lowdown on my personal business model

My business is a registered company called the Quick Shift Deva, Pty Ltd based out of South Africa, even though I have been travelling extensively for the last seven years. I am a professional life coach, international speaker, facilitator of workshops and corporate conferences, as well as a de-clutter expert. I am a multi-published author, run transformational and writing retreats around the world, and have worked extensively work within the YPO organisation.

I was basically operating an international business, as a one-woman show, for quite a while. In the last five years, nothing really changed other than that I no longer have a "home" base in South Africa. All the functionality, invoicing and payments within my business stayed exactly the same.

When I was in a particular location, I worked with clients face to face. For instance, when in South Africa I would do home or office clutter-clearing jobs, meet with clients face to face, be the keynote speaker for events or run retreats. When booked to host a retreat in another country, I might fly for the weekend to work in Italy or Dubai for the YPO. Or, when booked for facilitation, I might have to head off to Lagos or Ghana for a full week. It was fluid and easy. As long as I had the qualities outlined above – along with my raucous sense of humour and technology with me – business mostly carried on as usual.

As part of my work rhythm (read more about that in Lesson 5) I would also predetermine what retreats I would be hosting in which country, and build additional work around that. I remember the first year I was set to co-run a writing retreat in Greece, and while in Warsaw for the YPO earlier that same year, I happened to mention to one of the YPO Cypriot Chapter administrators that I was going to be in Greece. Going to work in Cyprus seemed like a no-brainer because, since I was going to Greece anyway, they had to fly me from Europe (lower flight prices) rather than from South Africa. In their mind, it was deemed a local budget-friendly flight rather than a long-haul international flight. And so, yes, I landed the job!

I would often make sure that different clients knew where I was going to be and when, to see if that could entice them to work with me. If you can find a way to lower expenses for your client, or pick them up yourself, then you have a winning combo. I also recall, once when I was in the USA for three months, that the YPO asked me to work in Dubai. I kid you not when I tell you that I was literally flying through Dubai the very same day they needed me to facilitate – en route to South Africa – so all I had to do was make a longer stop over and delay my flight out of Dubai for 24 hours. And, to top it all – *Bam!* – I landed another two jobs en route south. I had become an integral part of the YPO by being accredited internally as a Certified Forum Facilitator, which meant I was able to facilitate certain in-house training sessions for the chapters and their forums. They booked me for Forum Fundamental training and then put it out to the various forums that I was available the following morning. I was also able to facilitate a Super Charge session for a new forum that didn't have to pay additional transport costs because that had all been picked up by the training the day before. This is what I call "batching" my work and travel. Trying to add work in a certain location to make the most of it.

Planning ahead is as important as being flexible. If I kind of knew to which destination I was headed and when, it was easier for me to attract other work in the same area. Once, when I was in Greece with my mum, preparing for our next writing retreat, an opportunity came up to run a YPO retreat in Prague. My motto is usually: just say yes, and then figure out how to make it happen. This included leaving my mum in the village and travelling on my own across the island at 11 pm at night on treacherous roads to get to the airport!

Everything can be worked out – or, as Marie Forleo says, "Everything is figureoutable!"

Marketing

When I first heard about the concept of life coaching 17 years ago, I knew immediately that that was the essence of who I was and how I would show up in life. I had this vivid vision of me sitting on top of a mountain, or at the beach, with a laptop and a pair of earphones and coaching clients. I knew even then that there would be this location-free aspect to my business. It was just a case of bringing it to life in a relevant way for me at the right time.

When I lived permanently in South Africa, I had a huge network and community. I often spoke at local events, charity functions, was constantly out and about networking, meeting and connecting people. When shifting to being #LocationFree, you have to be mindful to pre-empt the notion of "out of sight, out of mind", which often kicks into gear. How do you manage that properly in order to stay top of clients' minds?

Because I was only in a particular country for a few months of the year, I had to be more discerning about what I booked ahead, to be more vigilant about connecting with important folk in my network when I was in that city. I could no longer rely on staying top of mind by being seen at events or workshops, so my online presence and visibility became a lot more important. As did my way of personally reaching out and connecting with clients when I was away from South Africa. (Read more about managing others in Lesson 9.)

I, for the most part, utilise the power of instant messaging, Facebook Messenger, Skype and WhatsApp to stay connected with clients around the world. When I am travelling and I think about them or see something they would love, I drop them a quick photo or message to say hi and reconnect. The personal touch. This has been a huge part of me keeping my network happy and engaged.

I ensure that I put a fair amount of time, energy and love into all my online branded portals. Regardless of whether your work is technology based, you will become more reliant on online platforms, because you are less visible on the ground.

My business starts with my social media presence, which in turn leads everyone to my website. I have certain short e-courses you can sign up for, to entice folk to register with me. They then get a series of emails on certain topics. For example, if you visit kate-emmerson.com you will find a free downloadable course titled "The Strategic Power of Disconnecting". Then, once someone signs up, I can send emails to him or her because they then fall under what

I call "traffic that I own". Although you may have the potential of influencing someone who follows you on Facebook, Instagram or LinkedIn, you don't "own that traffic" until they have agreed to share their email address with you. What is more, your social media accounts can be closed, blocked, locked down or hacked at any point, as has happened to many businesses. Imagine your Facebook page no longer exists because you have pissed off the powers that be? Always be circumspect about how much you trust and rely on technology – it is not foolproof. At the end of the day, your official subscribers – in other words, clients or potential clients whom have given you their email addresses – are the gold in your business. Look after them, connect with them, offer them amazing content – and don't take them for a ride. Make special offers, send sales emails and invite them to events, because they are now "part of your tribe".

From the get go, when I started my coaching business at the end of 2003, I always spoke about how I coached from anywhere and to anywhere. Back then we still had landlines and a dial-up internet connection in South Africa, but I was determined to share my "coach from anywhere" mind set and taught my clients that we did not have to work face to face. As a result, living and working #LocationFree was just another step along that trajectory because I had been educating and yakking on about this for eons.

Even when I was in the same city as my clients, I would still try to coach on the phone so that they didn't have to waste precious time getting to and from me. It was all in the way I sold it to them; I framed it as "better" and "just as effective", with "no waste" of time, money or energy. I also made it less expensive so that there was very real benefit to doing on a session online rather than face to face. It is all about how appealing you make something sound.

So if you find that you are encountering resistance from clients, I am going to strongly suggest that that resistance is actually within you. How can you shift what is going on inside so that you can buy into the idea that doing it via Skype, Zoom or even WhatsApp when necessary is going to be more than okay?

There is definitely a time and place for the warm and fuzzy feeling of face to face, or being in the same room, but that can be the cherry on the top. Or that can be reserved for VIP clients. Certain clients might never work online, or don't feel confident doing so, requiring more visual clues in order to trust you, or perhaps they don't feel safe talking from home, worried that someone may hear them.

Many of those who are unable to access you face to face will in fact opt for online communication. Not surprisingly, over the years, there were perhaps no more than two or three potential clients I have not been able to clinch because they refused or were unable to work remotely, and I just had to let them go. Not always easy, of course, but may be the price one has to pay. It also all goes back to the issue of trust – trusting that they were meant to work with someone better suited to their needs.

So, how you are going to conduct your business or work? Part of the fun of the process is figuring out how to do that in a way that works for you and your particular skill set, business model and client or employer requirements. No one size fits all!

Writing

I have always written in some form. When clients sign up for the free course I offer, they are also added to my newsletter. I have been writing this in various forms for the past 17 years. When I started out, I used to have to manually send the newsletter out to 10 email addresses at a time, because I didn't yet have automated software. I remember the day that I was able to sign up for the local-based business, Diamatrix, and start automating all my emails and subscriber newsletters. That was a day of celebration, realising the untapped potential of online leverage.

I started writing and selling online coaching courses back in 2004, but these too had to be manually sent to clients each week. Can you imagine manually sending emails for a course every Monday, Wednesday and Friday? It's laughable. Oh, the joy of being able to add someone to an automated system and then letting the program deliver all the course material? Heaven! Hallelujah! Automation was a game changer.

Nowadays, all of this is, of course, commonplace and normal – and also super affordable compared to 16 years ago. As a result, the barrier to entry is so much lower now.

Today there are all sorts of email delivery programs that boast sophisticated customer-engagement systems integrated with "lead scoring" for your clients, tagging systems and clever tricks to manage a better business, both online and face to face: programs such as ActiveCampaign, Infusionsoft and online teaching programs like Thinkific, Teachable, Kajabi and Udemy. Selecting one can be a bit of a minefield, so trust your gut, pick one and get good at using it. Or outsource to someone you trust and respect.

Social media

Utilising social media has been pivotal to my personal branding story, and right from the outset I was determined to learn how to navigate and optimise my personal Facebook profile, Facebook pages and groups, Instagram, Twitter, Linkedin, Google, and YouTube. You might make use of all of these or just some, your decision based on the requirements of business, your own preference and the profile of your clients and where they like to hang out.

I have found that I instinctively understand certain platforms more than others, so I spend more of my precious energy there; for example, I get Facebook but I don't get Twitter. So, while I have a Twitter account, I don't spend too much energy trying to figure it out. For me, it simply isn't worth the hassle – as wise folk always say: pick your battles! The same applies to other social media – pick one or two that resonate and get maximum traction out of them, rather than trying to cover them all and doing it badly.

Maybe your line of work is a little different, but I am always interested in finding the simplest way to do business in the smartest way possible. How to streamline and deliver effective solutions for ideal clients, and then learn and tweak as you go along.

Outsourcing

Part of being #LocationFree is knowing what to outsource so you get to appreciate the beautiful places you are living in. There isn't much point being in a wonderful location when you are glued to your desk 15 hours a day.

I think of myself as a small business with a big-ish income, small-ish expenses and some clever outsourcing.

Over the years I have at various times outsourced the following:
- **Accountant:** For the past 15 years I have paid for the services of a professional accountant.
- **Web design:** I don't ever want to have to learn how to design a website, so I have happily handed that responsibility to someone with the necessary skill and enthusiasm.
- **Assistant:** For several years, I have employed a virtual assistant. My first VA happened to live in the same city as me, but I wanted to start off in the way I wished to continue, so we worked virtually more than face to face. We would meet once a month, but did the rest over the phone or online via Dropbox. This meant that I got used to the idea of being in another country and still be able to have support when I needed it.
- **Public relations:** I have used PR effectively for specific projects, each of which had specific outcomes and fixed budgets.

- **Social media expertise:** Engaging experts in the field meant that I had the right help at the right time when launching certain books or projects.
- **Consultants:** When switching over to Infusionsoft, I paid to be properly coached in using the system so as to shorten my learning curve.

Although I use technology a lot in my business – and, being #LocationFree, you might expect everyone to be tech nerds – but let me assure you that I am not one of those naturally tech-minded folk! I find technology daunting and getting to grips with it hard rather than instinctive. I had to drag myself into learning technology that supports and facilitates my business model. I have to be shown something three times before I eventually get it, but then it's locked into my brain.

So when I switched to Infusionsoft, I realised I was not making the most of the expensive platform, and managed to find someone to help me use it better and make the most of the money I was paying for it. The same with Facebook adverts – at various times, I have paid for support and help so I don't have to be bogged down by it all.

For me, it all boils down to trying to break the typical entrepreneurial trap of being a jack of all trades and doing everything yourself. It's better business sense to know what you are brilliant at and play to your strengths. If you are being paid the highest rate to do XYZ, then what can you outsource to give you more time to utilise your strengths on XYZ? It's good to be able to do things yourself, be self-reliant and able to trouble shoot, but maybe you can gain even more traction by outsourcing some professional help along the way?

I tried various options along the way; some worked, while others didn't. One person may be ideal for one aspect and not for the next. Be willing to explore to stay curious. Don't get stuck doing everything yourself; free up time to love where you are living when #LocationFree – to explore and live, not be stuck running your business. Figure out what that means for you, and be willing to drop a little cash where needed to source the right help at the right time for the right reason.

Referrals

I have a huge network and am a great connector of ideas and people. I am instinctively able to connect people and, if I know I'm not the right coach or speaker for someone, I happily refer my client to the right person for the job. I have an open referral system in place that is casual rather than a fixed affiliate programme that has to work in a certain way. If someone passes work on to me, I am only too happy to pay them a finder's or referral fee or treat them to a fancy lunch as a thank-you gesture.

In the same vein, I allow others to do the same for me and gladly accept a referral commission for work passed on. I love the flow that it creates without being bound to it. I remember my first year of living #LocationFree … I had to pass up a lot of business opportunities because I was quite simply, physically, not in the right country at the right time and so passed the work on to someone I trusted and could recommend with confidence. And by the end of that year, all those referral commissions added up to the cost of an overseas trip. That is what I call "keeping the energy of money flowing".

Insurance

Insurance is a very personal issue, but because I tend to be a little clumsy and travel lot, the chances of things being broken, lost or stolen are pretty high. So, decades ago, I decided to get good insurance. I make sure I have public liability for me and solid all-risk coverage for my indispensible stuff: my computer, mobile phone, and prescription glasses and sunglasses. I also have excellent health insurance (*see* Lesson 7), so everything that matters is well insured and easy to replace wherever I am in the world. If something goes wrong, my broker in South Africa simply gets it sorted. It may occasionally be a pain in the ass to claim, of course. One year, in the little seaside village of Skala Eressos in Greece, I dropped my phone and that was that. Dead. To claim, I needed a police report, and that took four days. We had to drive to the next village to file the report, then it had to be translated by an official translator, which took yet another week, and only then could I file my claim in South Africa. Rather than the usual replacement phone that would otherwise be couriered to me, my broker was to reimburse the money directly into my account so I could buy a replacement in Greece. But, with all the legalities, by the time it was all processed, I was already back in South Africa for work and – *Voila!* – a replacement phone was delivered 24 hours after I landed. *Ta-dah!*

In the meantime, by being active on the village Facebook group, I had been offered the use of three phones – the power of being connected to the community in which you live.

Managing documents

The simple answer is: *back up* and then *back up again!*

Keeping your business and documents safe is vital – even more so when #LocationFree and on the move, because you don't have a standard desk, desktop or office from which to retrieve a document when needed.

Generally, you need a smart phone and a computer and some form of clever storage system, usually online, as well as physical hard drives.

Choose iCloud storage such as Google Docs or Dropbox, which are also great for shared access for both business and family. Be sure to have a good back-up system on an external hard drive too and, to be extra safe, put special documents on an additional flash drive. In fact, it's a good idea to have another fully backed-up hard drive in a separate location, which can be couriered if a document is lost or damaged along the way. And, if you work on a Mac, Apple Mac has a special system called Time Machine that does perfect computer replicas, so you can backtrack to a time in the past and recreate your entire machine over again.

I tend to travel with some paper-based documents. Depending on where I am travelling to, I might not be able to get workbooks printed or copies made. These might include notes for workshops, workbooks, retreat exercises, as well as travel documents. I carry a police clearance with me, copies of travel documents, plus personal mementos that are meaningful to me – all in gorgeous A4 envelopes. I might even have workbooks for writing retreats and language classes – in Spain I have a Spanish workbook – as well as personal retreats, coaching or family constellations.

I find it impossible to be 100% paper free, because I also love the texture and tactile nature of writing by hand and adore journals. I also do all my dreaming and envisioning in beautiful notebooks. I planned the entire outline of this book in two hours on 13 pages of a bright yolk-yellow notebook in Malaga! My initial thinking and planning had to be done by hand, on paper, because my heart and brain function better that way!

A final note of warning … Find the best way to keep documents practical, safe and accessible! Think duplicates and back ups as necessary from now on.

 **WHAT OTHERS SAY ABOUT …**

Running a global business

I have a few different hats that I'm wearing at the moment. One is that I'm a web developer and so I take on clients to work on web development projects. I am also in the middle of developing a wellness retreat aimed at the remote working community. This will bring mental wellness, physical wellness, nutrition and health topics over the course of a seven-day retreat and this is to make the remote lifestyle much more sustainable. I have found that a lot of nomads tend to be attracted to the Instagram lifestyle that this looks like online, but they fail to really define their purpose and they also let other practices become less sustainable, such as eating out a lot and not taking care of themselves. And so this retreat that myself and a partner are building will help them maintain these practices to make the lifestyle more sustainable. In terms of legalities and things like that, it depends on what country I'm in, but I have found that, with remote work, it's an area that's still evolving a lot and so if I'm doing anything in person, then I work on getting the proper visas and whatnot. However, if it's online then it just stays online.

—**Gene Ellis**

Sadly, this has been a bit of an error of better judgement arena for me. I have allowed my website to lapse, and when I was back home in December, I never managed to set up my work email on my phone before leaving South Africa again. These are mistakes that can cost you, so learn from me, make sure you have those accounts paid and allow for fluidity to take place, as you settle into the new chapter of your life. I have, however, remained very active on my Instagram account and this is linked to my Facebook page, so in a small way I am still in touch with my followers on there. This is also an area where you need to have a firm grasp of what you take along with you and what you wish to leave behind. If your business is one that has flowed into the next chapter, make sure you have all the necessary legal documents in place, passwords at hand, and logons at your disposal. Otherwise you will have a frustration that could have been avoided.

Link your accounts as soon as you can. Make sure your banking is online or, even better, on your mobile, so you have access to it at the push of a finger prompt. This can be a terrible setback if you don't have mobile-phone access back to your home country. I am currently earning money on international waters, on a ship that is registered in a flag port, which doesn't attract taxes. What this means for me is that my earnings are tax free. Currently, if I spend more than 183 days out of South Africa, my monies cannot be taxed. This legislation is currently under revision. Make sure that you are aware of the financial implications on your earnings, especially if you are transferring monies back to your birth or home country. There can often be tax issues regarding these monetary issues and you would rather be aware of these than be faced with these further down the line.

Try not to convert to your home currency. This can often lead to panic and mistrusting your earning ability and situation. My biggest frustration is having to go into the officers' pub and purchase a bottle of wine for $22. When I do the conversion back to South African rand at 15:1 or more, I then have to have a battle in my head. Trust me, it's not worth it. If you want something and you are earning in the foreign currency, look at that situation and be objective. If I need to justify sending R330 South African rand on a bottle of Sauvignon Blanc, I am not going to buy it. But when I think, I have earned $X today and I am taking $22 of those to celebrate my day, it really does sit just there, and doesn't become a guilt trip on a train ride to nowhere.

—Deborah Louise Botha

For a while, I remained a sole trader in the UK, because I knew the system, how to record sales and expense figures, and how to complete my tax return. Pre-Brexit, if we stayed fewer than 183 days in another EU country, then we didn't have to pay taxes to that country. For a while I subscribed to a UK mailing address and used my son's home address for all legalities and bank accounts. I invoiced clients in GBP and they credited my UK bank account via BACs as they always had done whilst I lived in England.

Then, whilst we were in Spain, it became certain that the UK would leave the EU. We had acquired our NIE number and temporary Residencia card in order to buy a Spanish-registered car, then to Brexit-proof ourselves further, needed to exchange our UK driving licences too.

Initially, when planning where to travel, I'd decided that Spain was not the best place to run a business, to be a sole trader, because it was quite expensive and complicated to negotiate the tax system. However, we had no plans to return to the UK and, after speaking with a Spanish accountant, the simplest way forward was to become an Autonomo. After all, we'd decided to make Spain our home base, so certainly wanted to contribute to the economy. Paying Spanish taxes also ensures we are eligible to access the state health service.

I use my euro debit card for purchases in Spain and to withdraw cash from the ATM. If shopping online, then it's often best to use my GBP card. My most difficult task was finding professional indemnity insurance here in Spain, because the concept of a virtual assistant just isn't recognised. Insurance providers just couldn't understand that I was working from home and didn't use nor require office space. After a number of conversations and completion of many proposal forms, I managed to find a policy, but it was more costly than the cover I had in the UK.

Everyone's circumstances will be different, so careful research into and consideration of the best options for operating a business and paying taxes needs to be done. I'd considered setting up a limited company in the UK, also in Bulgaria where the tax is a very low 10%, and also becoming an *e-resident in Estonia. It was a hard choice to accept I needed to trade from Spain, but then I had no control over Brexit.*

—Nancy Benn

One part of my business is to teach seminars (Jikiden Reiki and Chi Nei Tsang) as well as spiritual healing. Both I can do wherever I am. Actually, where to go often has to do with where people want me to teach. And my online consultations are venue independent. The second part is my network business with cellular nutrition, something I do 80% online and the other 20% wherever I am.

The only important thing is to always have a good internet connection for everything; apart from that, I am totally free where to go. I have an official tax address, which is due to my cellular nutrition business. For seminars etcetera, it depends on whether they are in Spain or abroad and, tax wise, can be handled through the centres that organise them for me.

—Nabila Welk

In my business, Scully Scooters, I enabled previously employed personnel to be suppliers to me (and others). This really helped with accountability. As far as possible, I make sure that we are working toward a plan and not, as is so often found in business, spending time mainly fighting fires or on the back foot. I focus on what has to happen, not all of the noise that surrounds it. Everyone knows what needs to be done and we use a CRM system to track the activity and tasks. We meet online, with an agenda, once a week or fortnight, depending on the circumstances. Stay connected but don't be in a state of "always available". Articulate this clearly to your team.

My other work is leading experiences for an experiential travel company called Unsettled. They are experts at living and working remotely. I was hired remotely. Many of our team have only ever met online and technology makes this all possible. Here, too, we all work together on a prepopulated plan.

I find that I am far more productive when working remotely than when I was in an office environment and, to top it all, I live a far more balanced and full life.

My accounting system, Xero, handles multi-currency so it's not very different from doing local business and paying taxes in the country where your business is registered, in my case South Africa.

—Lynne Scullard

We have multiple online stores, selling art and photography products. The online stores are usually drop-shipment models, which is best for us as we don't have to carry inventory. We file our Canadian taxes each year. We use our debit cards at the ATMs.

—Chris de Cap

I champion and support mission-driven entrepreneurs and tame their unruly businesses. I run accountability programmes, workcations and retreats, so being in a sunny climate helps where we can get outside instead of just doing the work is priceless. Walking meetings are amazing in the sunshine.

My other company is online business design and strategy where my team and I build and automate businesses. I specifically chose that route as I wanted to work location free, plus I get to meet some really interesting characters as clients too.

My advice is to try to charge in one currency and make it the currency you're registered to pay tax in. Makes things a lot easier at the end of the year.

—Carolynne Alexander

I am an author and SEO copywriter. I'm lucky enough to work for and with companies that are used to outsourcing their work – they will hire programmers from Ukraine or graphic designers from India, so hiring a copywriter in Spain is easy. If anything, it gives us something to break the ice with when jumping on a call: "So, what's the weather like over there?" Since I'm a resident in Spain and spend the bulk of my time here, I am tax-eligible in Spain. This is where I pay my taxes. Fortunately, all my clients are in the euro zone, so there are no currency-exchange issues. Clients pay their bills to me via bank transfers.

—André Gussekloo

With investing, sometimes I end up having to work nights, depending on what time zone I'm in. There are definitely issues when the internet or phone service is unreliable. Most of the stuff is online so no issues for me. With currency, it's best to withdraw from ATMs or to exchange (depends on the country). Good to use $100 bills to get the best exchange rate. And, when using an ATM, don't let them convert into your currency. They'll screw you. Your bank probably won't. Don't exchange at the airport if you can help it.

—Uday Jhunjhunwala

I'm a business and media mentor. I see living location independent as a positive way to run my business, as most of my clients are online. I have relevant advisors who I work with in Spain and the UK. Client billings and payments are generally made in the UK, where the majority of my clients are.

—Victoria Jane Watson

I don't have a business; I have a number of part-time jobs. The main one is housesitting, for which I ask travel costs and a small day fee, which covers my costs.

Also, since last year, I have a job as a mountain-hiking travel guide with a Dutch travel company, for which I will guide hiking vacations of one or two weeks, with eight to 15 guests. These are scheduled quite far in advance, so I just plan the housesitting jobs around it.

And, lastly, I have been giving sushi workshops for 10 years now, doing a couple of workshops a month for a sushi restaurant/company in Holland. Since I started travelling, I will only do the workshops during the times I am in the vicinity of Amsterdam. Luckily, the company is quite flexible with regard to my being away for long periods, which is really nice, as this part-time job is still a nice addition to my life.

I just pay my regular taxes in my home country, on the income of my jobs. Currencies are also not a big issue as most of Europe has the same currency (euro).

The biggest organisational issue in getting into the house-less way of living was actually finding a way to stay registered in the national registration system, which in the Netherlands is the basis of all institutions. In 99,99% of the cases, it is "living at address XYZ", but in my case it is a postal address. This was hard to get organised as councils in the Netherlands are yet unfamiliar with this way of living and don't have a suitable registration for it. So after I got that organised, I immediately started getting letters from my insurance company, for instance, needing to check whether I was still eligible for the Dutch health-insurance system, etcetera. And another pretty hard thing to do was finding suitable travel insurance that suited my needs - in other words, also covered my activities like housesitting and volunteer work and health insurance coverage abroad if necessary.

—**Martin van den Berg**

I sell online courses in Danish and English, have clients on Zoom in both languages and sell books in both too. Living globally means that some clients won't choose me, while others will choose me for that. In the big picture, I don't really think it matters. I do my best in every area without struggling and trust that I will get what I need.

I am somewhat dependent on good internet and being in rough places with raw, untouched beauty makes that a challenge. I am trying to manage a balance, so I get my fix of untouched and some time with good internet for my clients. I use Stripe and PayPal. I am based in Colombia and they have no additional tax on digital products or services. I don't mind paying tax and always paid the 40%-plus tax in Denmark with pleasure, but of course it gives me more freedom to not pay anything extra for a while on the digital products.

—Mette Glargaard

I'm an accountant and I own my own business. It's a very stable business; customers tend to stay for years. I still have on board all the same customers I started with some six or seven years ago. My company is registered in Finland and I pay all my taxes there. We live in Spain through a European Union arrangement called the A1 certificate, which defines your fiscal country of residence despite where you spend your time. All my accounting customers are Finnish companies, but my clients are a very international bunch because a lot of them are originally from another country. A lot of my customers travel a lot for work too. We hardly ever see each other, and all documents are transferred virtually. We communicate via email, phone calls, WhatsApp and Skype.

—Katia Enbuske

Based in community development and engagement consultancy, training and facilitation, the lifestyle suits my work well. I'm one of the founding members of the Jeder Institute, a boss-less collective of approximately 40 people (mainly Australia based) and we have a finance company that looks after our needs and does everything for me.

There are only two of us who do more of this international work, but most of them are Australia based. But because of our expansion and our growth, we've had to look for an organisation that will look after all of that and knows currency exchange and taxes because Australia has GST and other countries do not. We asked around in our own networks, in our own field, "Who would you recommend? Who would understand the way we work?" So, yeah, we found someone who can do that and this company who is now looking after us also has dispersed leadership.

—**Dee Brooks**

 **WHAT OTHERS SAY ABOUT ...**

The highs and lows in business

My business low point was losing non-VAT registered UK clients as my support suddenly became more costly due to having to charge Spanish IVA tax. My invoices now have to show the total in euros, but I include GBP for my UK clients who can still credit my English bank account. I then transfer living funds each month to my current account in Spain. I invoice my US client in dollars via PayPal, and then move the funds to Transferwise before transferring to my bank account.

A high point? I'd informed my clients that I'd be taking a holiday in September 2017, but not that I wouldn't be returning to the UK. After a couple of weeks working remotely in Spain, after proving that I could provide uninterrupted support, I then notified my clients where I was in a few interesting and funny conversations! They were amazed, but did confirm that they may have panicked a little that I'd been unable to work efficiently if they'd known of my plans beforehand.

—**Nancy Benn**

I've had many, many of both!

A business high would be getting investors for a business project that I was working on and that was a really pivotal moment. It allowed us to scale up our team, allowed us to really execute our vision. There was a business a friend and I were running. We had taken on investors and had agreed we could get several rounds of funding from them. So we received the first round of funding at a certain valuation that really allowed us to scale the business, hire employees. Business was great - we were signing really big contracts. And then we went back for our second round of funding from them and the investors wanted to renegotiate the valuation. And this didn't make sense because the company was profitable. It didn't make sense that the investors wanted to renegotiate their valuation, saying that it's gone down. Long story short, the investors insisted on a much lower valuation for the second round of funding, which would have given them 51% of the company. They then said that, after this round of funding closes, they intended on taking their 51% and firing all of the staff of the company and making myself and my co-founder work for them. And that was definitely a business low. And then we said, "Well, we will just not take your round of funding." And then they said, "We will sue you to make you take our round of funding." And so that was a very, very low point of the business. We essentially lost the company and now were becoming employees to our investors. Definitely a business low.

The business high was that this happened on a Friday night and so my partner and I said, "Well, we need to go to court against our investors,

but we don't have the money to fight them." *And so that evening we said,*
"Let's just get on the phone and call anyone - friends, family, business
associates, anyone that's willing to support our crowd-funding campaign
for our legal defence against our investors."

By Monday morning we had verbal commitments for over one million
dollars and we called up our investors and said, "We will gladly see you in
court. We have a million-dollar war chest to fight you on this." So that
was definitely a business high. In the end, the investors backed down;
they were eventually bought out. And, unfortunately, this whole scenario
really killed the momentum of the company so eventually the company was
folded, but it was definitely a business high to take them on in that sense.

A business low would be before that and having run my bank account
down to literally $5 and thinking about how I can spread that out over
a few days in terms of having food to eat. However, I'm not sure if I'd
call that a low. It was just a defining moment because it really caused
me to take a hard look at what I was willing to sacrifice for a dream
basically. And having that kind of experience of being down to your last
couple dollars by choice because of not wanting to just jump back into the
regular workforce, it really helped to show myself that I was willing to
risk everything to maintain the dream of running a business. So a business
high is definitely getting funded. A business low is when you leverage
everything and sometimes that doesn't work out.

—*Gene Ellis*

A business high for me is the people I have met. This is such a pool of
diversity and cultural richness, which often leads to the most hysterical
situations of miscommunication and a wonderful life of discovering that
life is not always as you see it or know it. When you can truly sit in the
company of the leagues of nations and understand and embrace each

other, you find life can be exceptional. Business done at this level can be frustrating and take longer than it would normally, whilst you navigate through language and different laws, but it can also be very rewarding. What you finally land up with is something that represents all parties, from all corners of the world, and they all have a voice in the project and results that are expected. This level of business is truly liberating and powerful. And, might I add, I believe it is the way business will be framed in the future.

The low is that you are often on your own. You need to be well versed and able to hold your own in a global environment. You might have another more dictator kind of personality that is in a higher position, who isn't used to being challenged or to thinking in a way that is different from theirs.

Often your time zone is different to your support systems back home, so if it can't wait, you might be required to decide without the safety net of referring to your team back home. This is okay too, because you hone your skills to relying on your own intuition more and, in situations like this, we grow.

I have learned more about me, as a friend to myself, a companion and a woman who has learned to appreciate her own company. The nomadic feeling of being liberated to make decisions, travel where I want to, commit to plans that I only need to consider for my own comfort and growth. This is a deep dive into your own person and what that means to you, and then the world in your sphere of influence. You learn to journey with yourself, as a friend and companion, not a rival. That has been my biggest realisation. I chose to journey on into an unknown space, but I took me with. Together we travel, together we teach, together we miss home.

—Deborah Louise Botha

High: I get to permanently teach new people in person, which is brilliant and very beneficial for all parts of my business and also personal growth.

Low: For my healing work, I prefer a certain setup, which is best if you have your fixed space. When travelling, it can be a bit complicated or better said, not as comfortable or as nice as I would like to have it.

You learn to be flexible and able to find solutions for whatever challenge is crossing your path.

—**Nabila Welk**

My recent business high was when an important client of mine in South Africa called a physical meeting with me. They were unaware that I was in Colombia, so I was in a predicament. I managed to get a colleague to attend physically and I called in via Zoom. It worked out perfectly.

My low was when I was in Bali a few years ago and a business partner stole a lot of money from the business. I think, however, that the reason I was able to catch him was that I was remote. Had I been in town there would have been too much "noise" and time to manipulate things and it may have taken me a lot longer to catch him.

My biggest take-away is to own your data. Be the administrators on all of your systems. Take time to set them up so that you can see everything and control who can do what.

—**Lynne Scullard**

I guess a high would be that even if work is stressful or busy, I'm often doing it from the pool or the beach.

—**Uday Jhunjhunwala**

The highs ... Meeting new people and exploring new places. I get bored fairly easily (typical entrepreneur) and it's the reason why I upped and left England. Also, I'm sunshine powered, so it's made such a difference to my mental health too.

The lows and the insight ... You take yourself with you. Any chinks in your armour will be exposed. You will face some really quiet and lonely times, when you have time to think, and this is the time to face your demons. It's transformative because we normally fill our lives with "stuff" and entertainment. When you're sat on a flight for a few hours or you're alone on a Friday night, it really makes you evaluate things. It's difficult, but you really do come back stronger.

Being a little older also means that you don't have to participate in everything that your "gang" is doing. I'm quite happy to be a little boring sometimes. I'm pretty happy with my own company.

—*Carolynne Alexander*

A high, I would say, is landing my hiking travel-guide job last year, which is a lovely addition to my already enjoyable life. And I am lucky enough to say that I really have not experienced any [business] lows. I have not [yet] been cancelled on by planned housesitting jobs in a way that put me on the spot, or been confronted with housesitting situations that were completely different from their profile/description or something. Again, maybe this is not a matter of encountering "lows", but a matter of accepting things as they cross my path, without putting on labels like "highs" and "lows", but just making the best of things. Life is not about what happens to you, but about how you respond to it.

—*Martin van den Berg*

Publishing my first book in 2009 and see it become a bestseller in three months was brilliant. I wrote a simple book about self-esteem and no one had done that before in Denmark, so it was in high demand.

A low was publishing my first novel in English on Amazon and see it sell ... nothing. I guess people saw me more as a psychotherapist. It got great reviews, but still didn't sell a lot. It discouraged me from writing fiction for a few years, but now I am back, writing a follow-up to the first novel.

Be as visible as you can about everything. I live a life that most only dream about and I can give them a little taste by talking about it - all aspects of it. That sells. I sell.

—Mette Glargaard

Accounting is a very good business model for a Digital Nomad. Once you get the business going, you don't have to spend much time marketing and your monthly income is quite stable. My customers respect my time and expertise: I call my own hours and I do the job with deadlines I have given to my customers and I expect them to cooperate with that time frame. The tax office has monthly deadlines we have to meet and I'm always planning my work well ahead to avoid having to work overtime or long days. When choosing your field of business, it's important to think about your work schedule: do you prefer to work during daytime, in the evening or at night? I never work past 5 pm and usually don't start working before 9.30 am. I only work three to four hours a day, sometimes just two hours, or I take a day off. I never work on weekends. Some 12 to 20 hours of work per week are enough for me to make a decent living.

Having a billing level of Finland and spending most of the money in Spain helps a lot with the equation. When I take a holiday, I have an assistant in Finland who does part of my work so that I don't get behind in deadlines.

Right now, I'm studying business and life coaching and launching a side business helping people with achieving their big dreams, like becoming *location independent or starting their own business. It's possible with a bit of planning and time. It may require studying a new profession or coming up with a savvy online business idea.*

—Katia Enbuske

One business high is how much of a positive impact being location independent has had on my professional network. I have found myself with a network of mentors and entrepreneur friends who I don't think I would have met if I had stayed in the UK. I think this is the biggest benefit of being location independent as you open yourself up to creating a limitless global community.

—Victoria Jane Watson

My company and even my customers are based in the Netherlands, so invoicing, costs and taxes are all there.

A business high for me is the annual subscriptions for making backups and updates. I have to make one sales effort to sell a subscription and then I keep the customer for years. While the costs of a one-month subscription is low, the customer is very easily convinced and after that the relationship exists for many years and I can still invoice every month!

—Jan van Kuijk

I think this lifestyle is just going to continue and so new products are going to come up all the time, which makes thing helpful. So let me go back and say I conceived this idea even before I came here – this idea of working as a virtual coach. I was in London in 2008 maybe and I did a training programme with a wonderful woman who shared a story about how she had a few years prior been diagnosed with cancer and needed to stop doing face-to-face work because she needed to attend to herself and her health. And so she shifted all her clients to virtual clients. And, as she shared that story, I took my pen and made a note, "Shifted all my clients to virtual clients" and underlined that and said, "Well, that's what I've got to do now – I've got to shift this work virtually."

And I had a couple of occasions in South Africa. Back in those times it was not comfortable for people to work online and we didn't have a strong enough internet connection to make that a sexy option. So I had one great occasion when I missed a plane to go to some remote town where I was meant to do some coaching, came back home, called the guy and said, "Let's do this on the phone." And he said, "Can we?" And I said, "You bet. We're going to do this on the phone."

And that was the start of me starting to ask all my clients, "Can we do this on the phone?" And, of course, we've now switched to video so it's very intimate. And when I did come here to Chile, I had a couple of face-to-face clients and I said to them, "I'll be back in three months. Do you mind if, for this three-month period, we do this on Skype or Zoom or whatever?" And they said, "Great." And when I didn't go back, I said, "Do you mind if we continue to do this online?" And we've just continued that way. So I'm delighted that my clients find me virtually and they're comfortable to work with me virtually.

One of the things I did learn, which would've been great if I'd learned right in the beginning, is to stop apologising for it. So in the beginning I would say, "I'm so sorry I'm not in your city. Are you okay if we work this way?" Now I don't say that at all; I say, "Thanks so much for being in touch, Kate. Would you meet me at 2 pm on Zoom? Here's your link. Lovely." And no one comes back and says, "Well, why can't you come to my city?" They meet me on Zoom.

It's about one's confidence in this space. I'm super confident in the virtual space and I'll make you feel comfortable. So no more apologies any more. This is just how it works. And I almost embed that for myself. I *actually search for service providers that work virtually as well because we're all aligned in how we work. Supporting others who work like me so that we can grow stronger in our ability to do that and create great products for people no matter where they are.*

—Michelle Clarke

It's a lot easier than you think it is. There are so many others who are doing this. By starting in a Digital Nomad hub, you will make a lot of new friends, some of them for life, and they will tell you all you need to know about lesser-known destinations you want to visit and they might have been to.

—André Gussekloo

There's one thing I'd like to share about the high because it seems almost meaningless to some people, but it meant so much to me. I was on a train from Slovenia to Austria and I was then heading to the airport and heading back to Australia. And I'd been with a whole group of friends from around the world who had an international gathering in Slovenia.

The night before we'd all had a big party and I had a few euro left in my wallet and I gave it all to the barman and said, "I don't need this any more, I'm flying home. Here's a good tip for you." Gave him everything that was left in my wallet. I get on this train and got myself settled and thought, "Right, I'm going to get a bottle of water and a white wine, a bit of a hair of the dog after last night."

I went up to the carriage and this big European guy is standing there, and I said, "Can I get a bottle of water and a wine?" He put it up on the bench, and I got my card out to pay for it and Boris (his badge said Boris) looks at me, points to the wall behind him and says, "Cash only." I almost cried. "I haven't got any." And he just put the bottles back down underneath.

"Oh my God, what am I going to do for four hours with not even a drink?" A sign on the toilet says, "Do not drink this water from the taps", and so I go back to the cabin and I'm trying to just kind of compose myself. "This is okay. I can deal with this." But you know you get the shaky lip and a bit of the wobbles. This lady across from me asked, in very broken English, if I was okay. "No." I started crying. "No water." She reached into her wallet and she took out four euros and she handed it to me: "Go. Water." "Thank you. Thank you." It was the kindest gesture from a stranger that I still obviously feel so much heart about.

You think, it wasn't a million dollars – it wasn't a private jet – she gave me four euros to buy some water and it was just magic. We spoke through her broken English for the next three hours about all kinds of stuff, laughing when we didn't understand each other. She gave me some muesli bars from her handbag for food and it was just the most wonderful trip.

A low would be when I had a small panic attack in the middle of an Indonesian street because it sunk in that I had no home. It was early on in the journey and in the middle of three weeks of back-to-back work across different regions of Indonesia. My work take-away from this was that my schedule was too packed and not enough rest time had been allocated; my personal insight was that refocusing on myself and my breathing and not my surroundings is the best way to ground myself anywhere in the world.

—**Dee Brooks**

 **TOP TIPS!**

- Anything is possible ... You can dream up a million ways to run *your* business or work from anywhere.
- For objective and inspirational support, participate in a Mastermind group.
- Keep it simple and make sure that all your business affairs, tax and legalities are in order.

The Zap of Zen: Routine, ritual and rhythm

SPENDING A LOT OF TIME away from what one would otherwise consider "normal" home life requires the ability to nurture your relationship with yourself. To ensure you activate the ability to feel self-nourished and use every trick up your sleeve to remain centred, connected, loving and loved. And that, of course, requires a different type of vigilance. Because it can – and does – go a little pear-shaped!

I consider one of my saving graces the intentional use of *routines* and *rituals* that tie into a bigger *rhythm*, and they became even more important when living #LocationFree. Everything I did had to be executed with more clarity, focused intention and quiet mindfulness than ever before.

There seemed to be less room for mucking about, less room for winging it, less time for self-pity (otherwise, I would sail beyond the "24-hour wallow" we discussed in Lesson 4). Once these three Rs were in place, I could easily kick up my heels and wing it for the rest of the time. But one needed to supersede the other. If I found that I was drifting, becoming too much laissez-faire, had sunk into a holiday mode of "do whatever", my moods, stability and sense of wellbeing would rapidly corrode. I am not suggesting that it will be like that for you, but sharing how it was – and occasionally still is – for me.

For purposes of clarity and understanding the difference between the three Rs and how they work together, below is a short explanation.

- **Routine** is something practical in its application, increases efficiency, is usually repetitive and, over time, becomes a pretty well-oiled, non-negotiable habit. It's built into one's lifestyle. In that way, it doesn't require too much thinking, preparation or self-negotiation, because it becomes unconscious competence. It just happens because of all the hard work you have put into making that routine an active part of your everyday life.

- **Ritual** has a much greater purpose and impact and implies doing things that give one a spiritual connection, inner warmth and purpose, and a deeper sense of meaning. I see rituals as a way to tap into the unseen forces at play, into the emotion of love, and to connect you to the possibility of everything. It doesn't necessarily have to be religious, but it will probably have spiritual significance for you. Rituals are usually small, intentional and purposeful actions, feelings and thoughts.

- **Rhythm** is the cadence of timing. It's the flow and energy with which you approach each day, week, month, year or decade. About interpreting timing and flow, energy and replenishment. I often use the concept of "work vibration", especially when it comes to business, referring to how you want the rhythm of your work week and year to unfold before you.

Implementing all three together allows me to keep my head screwed on, stay aligned and focused, and continuously integrate a sense of normalcy in my travelling life. It definitely didn't work *all* the time, but mostly it did and still does for me. When we embark on holiday or travel for a few nights away for business, our personal routine and good habits can fall by the wayside. It's easy to let yourself off the hook for short digressions from routine and habits. Less exercise, yummy new food, late nights and more alcohol than usual are par for the course. Yet I found that when moving around continuously *is* your way of life, that same implementation of routine becomes vital for self-preservation, mental health and a sense of being "at home" every day. It has to be inbuilt, automatic and non-negotiable. It has to matter to you – to also make a significant difference to your energy and outlook. Your personal rituals and routine are often the only continuous thread you have in order to stay tapped in and connected.

Routine

I briefly discussed aspects of this idea when we covered "settling in" in Lesson 2. Because of my minimal lifestyle and paired-down capsule wardrobe, unpacking and settling in at that very practical level is pretty simple for me. When it comes to travelling, unpacking and settling in, packing up, moving and settling in again, a few routines kick into gear. For shorter-term stays of up to four nights, my routine is that I unpack what I need for that specific stay. Sometimes I might be able to pre-pack at the last destination in such a way that just my small carry-on luggage holds everything I need for that particular trip, and my bigger case can remain locked and unopened. However, if I were staying between four days and up to two weeks, I remove everything I need for that longer stay. It might depend on the location, as well as the time of year and the season or weather. For example, if I were delivering a retreat in the bushveld, I wouldn't necessarily unpack my beach gear and shorts.

I remove everything I need from my suitcases, pack it away beautifully into the cupboards and drawers, and then lock up everything else into the suitcases and place them far out of the way, on top of a cupboard. An even better trick is to ask to store my suitcase out of my room or apartment, so as not to have that "suitcase lurking" in my sight. There is something deeply psychological about having a suitcase constantly in view. It's unsettling and unnerving and makes everything feel temporary, the very opposite of everything I hope to achieve by my routine, which is to settle in and feel grounded.

In other scenarios, if I was working generally online with clients, perhaps writing my own manuscript in a small Greek village, or running a retreat for two weeks, I might unpack only all my casual beach- or sportswear: a big hat, sandals, my bathing suit and sarong. Stuff that is light, easy to wash and wear in hot beach locations, allows me to jump on a bike with ease and get sand between my toes with no problem. If I were in a city but with no big corporate workshop booked, I wouldn't necessarily unpack my fancy corporate skirts, jackets and suit attire. Those might stay in the suitcase, but I would unpack more semi-casual clothes.

So my routine is that, if staying for only two weeks, I remove on average only two-thirds of my suitcase. But when I know I'll be staying put in one location for more than two weeks, I unpack everything. Everything. And clean my suitcase for good measure. Part routine, part healthy habit to air all my clothes, and part personal trick to help me feel perfectly at home with a more well-rounded wardrobe. It also means that, at any given time, I know every wearable item of clothing, shoes, scarves, jewellery that I owned. That's also a great way to ensure you do *not* keep buying impulsively – especially when in a new country with an array of appealing shops.

Ritual

I use rituals to bookend my day: a way of greeting the morning and closing it out at night. I consider this "ritual" rather than "routine" because it is all about *feeling* better and *feeling* connected. Of course, it might vary slightly, depending on country, location and weather, but part of being able to feel at *home* wherever I am is instilling and following some of my own self-care rituals. I like and need little life hacks for my itinerant lifestyle.

I usually start the day with some lemon squeezed in water – so much so that once when I was in Cyprus for four nights to work with the YPO, I asked my hostess to bring me five fresh lemons when she came to greet me. It instantly puts me at ease knowing I can start the day just how I like to! Or else, I will drink plain hot water while waiting for my first coffee to brew. Because, let's face it, what I *really* want first is coffee, but my body goes on something of a rebellious streak if I do too much caffeine too often. And once one little innocent coffee is safely down the hatch, it always wants a friend. A little like tequila, I guess, just more socially acceptable at 6 am! So I try to offset the coffee with cleansing hot water before it's too late and my eyes are wide.

Another part of my daily ritual is some form of exercise, mediation or yoga. Most mornings I will either go for a cycle, a walk or do some yoga in my room or apartment at the very start of the day. My body's natural clock generally wakes me at 6 am. If there are no yoga classes I can attend, I practise yoga on my own. I also like to use an awesome yoga app, Down Dog, which is downloaded onto my phone. You can set classes from 15 minutes right up to 75 minutes with a variety of yoga styles (Full practice, Ashtanga, Hatha, Restorative), music choice, along with male or female voices to guide your practice and speed, for instance. I can thus vary routines in order to alleviate boredom, but at least I know that first thing in the morning I can get my Zap of Zen. But in truth, depending on where I am, a walk on the beach in fresh air followed by a long swim is my preferred exercise. Followed by sitting quietly at the water's edge in quiet inner reflection.

I also have a ritual of morning journaling. This is a process I started at the age of 13 and have developed over the years since. This is what Julia Cameron coined as "Morning Pages". It is a stream of unconscious writing, usually soon after you awaken and are not yet *in* your day. It is a very effective way of dumping down your thoughts. I have used this a lot in my coaching and retreats, where we do a massive "dump" out of the head and onto the page or computer at the start of the process. Once out of the head, it can be far more readily addressed and dealt with. I *love* morning journaling in the quiet of the day, before the rest of the world wakes up – a few pages penned while sipping freshly brewed coffee.

In the evening I call on a few things to close off the day, from reading a non-work-related book, to quiet contemplation, to writing. Often I can simply crawl into bed and lie there quietly, mulling over my day with gratitude and love. But, if I am feeling highly stressed and off kilter and travelling alone, I may need a little more structure to wind down.

Whenever I go through a particularly rough patch, I might resort to one of the smart phone apps designed to help you switch off, rest deeply and sleep peacefully. I have a variety at my disposal so use what I most intuit will work that particular night. It might be a guided meditation, an inner-calm breathing exercise or a "better sleep" hypnosis app. I use different ones as and when appropriate and try to not get sucked into that rabbit hole of having *every* available app on my phone because those are just distractions and confusing clutter.

My use of apps is ironic, I know, because I am an *ardent* proponent of less and less active screen time and constant numbing out by staring at a blue screen. But, with these apps, you can simply lie in bed and listen to them as you drift off to sleep.

At other times my ritual, depending on time zones, might be to chat to a friend to stay connected across the water. I also sometimes get stuck into a Netflix movie, or find something to laugh at on YouTube, for example, but my main aim on most nights is to *not* rely on my screen keeping me entertained.

Another component of ritual for me is the small altar I set up. I have a few treasures that always travel with me and have a precious meaning. Most have been given to me by my friends, family and loved ones. This is a way of reserving a small space for focused gratitude and energy. A collection of significant small objects: a candle, a wish box, special jewellery, a small crystal, a miniature Buddha and cow statue, thread from a special retreat, heart-shaped rocks from my beloved island Iona and even a paper flower. I need no more than a small space to create a circle of love around me and this is my way of feeling closely connected to my loved ones. I also have decks of cards for inspiration and insight – like a word for the day, or a lovely spiritual reminder. The little circle I call my altar is my visual Zap of Zen. Do you have the same in your home? And how would you create that for yourself when travelling?

Rhythm

For me, rhythm is all about the bigger picture. What is the intentional focus? Where do you place your attention? What is the vibration like?

Rhythm is about the annual ebb and flow you create between work and play, and how you factor in work commitments or deadlines alongside family, friends and much-needed down time. It is also about weather and seasons and what ignites you at different times of the year.

At the beginning of every year, for the past 15 years, I have created a vision board. The actual process is covered extensively in my book *Ditch Your Glitch*. In this beautiful and creative process, I determine an intentional word or short powerful sentence as the overall *theme* of the year to come. This is the overriding intention that drives and feeds everything. It determines the "colour", look and feel of the year's rhythm. It determines what I say yes to, and what I say no to. It impacts business and personal decisions from the get go. Everything I choose to focus on will be assessed in relation to the rhythm of the year. What's the *one* overriding theme and how is everything I purposefully do aligned to that theme's rhythm?

I also make time to map out the year in terms of where I need to travel to, given current and upcoming work obligations. And then I engage with family and friends to figure how and where I will connect with them. I also build in pockets of rest when I am looking at the flow of my year. Pockets to rejuvenate. After a big retreat or a demanding work obligation or talk, I make sure that there is sufficient down time. I constantly try to put *less* on the schedule rather than more, looking at broader brush strokes in terms of achievements and my own personal success thermometer.

I have, for the most part, learned to visit countries in three-month silos or slots. That allows me to feel as though I can breathe, rest and be in between all the doing, working and travelling. The result is a perfect rhythm and balance that works for me. What works best for you? Or what might work when you give it a bash? In my first year of #LocationFree I was like a buzzing bee – here, there and everywhere. But I learned fast that disrupting my rhythm and the resulting exhaustion was going to be the end of me. (*See* The LAY Principle in Lesson 8.)

To maintain a rhythm requires planning ahead. I have realised more and more that people plan big overseas trips about a year in advance and that helped my business partner, Sarah, and I plan our international retreats earlier. Of course, all those good intentions went to pot in 2020 because we ended up having to reschedule and push them all out by a year. But preplanning also helped me understand when or whether to agree to work in another country.

For example, when I knew I was going to be in USA, I wouldn't say yes to work back in South Africa. Even contemplating the possibility would throw my rhythm out of whack.

The saying that epitomises my thinking is: The juice just isn't worth the squeeze. Unless the fee for the job was at my top-end rate, there is a hefty portion for travel, and ticks other criteria boxes, I won't even consider it. There are many reasons. One, because I know the effect and impact on my body and energy. This might sound arrogant, but it really is more about self- preservation and self-care – crossing too many time zones and all that airplane travel wreaks havoc. Secondly, I preferred to immerse myself in *one* place rather than be constantly on the move. Thirdly, carbon footprint is always something to consider and too much back and forth is not environmentally sound.

It was a different story before living #LocationFree … I would hop all over the place, but could then also go "back home" to my safe little space and my cat to rest and recharge. Being #LocationFree requires a different approach, however. This is simply what worked for me, of course, so be sure to read others' experiences about what works for them. You also can't expect what works at the beginning to continue to work year in and year out. But I do love the concept I call *batching* – keeping like with like. Staying in one country and working there, or nearby, rather than travelling back and forth.

For me, this idea of rhythm and batching also links into how we allocate our time and space. I love to batch certain tasks together. For example, do all my sales calls in the morning and all marketing in the afternoon, or all meetings or out-of-office tasks on certain days. When I am travelling I try to avoid working while on the go; I prefer to use travel as personal reading and dreaming time. I hate working on planes and in airports unless it's an absolute emergency and, let's face it, *real* emergencies are few and far between.

Essentially, my rhythm is mapped out at the beginning of each year, and I try to stick to it. I have had to start saying no to a lot of potential opportunities, learn to be more discerning. Really *living* what I teach – in other words, to let go, de-clutter, prioritise quality over quantity, and stick to my plan of the location I was in. The less-is-more, less-is-vital philosophy.

I think I only really got that right after feeling the burn-out effects of travel: as much as my heart and soul were loving the vibe, my body took a lot longer to catch up. For someone who has always been a Duracell bunny of energy, I had to start looking after my energy a whole lot better. So I started batching countries better and better, or at least adjacent ones. And because I was teaching the art of letting go and saying no, I had to put this into action and pass up more than half opportunities, unless they were online!

Another component of what I build into the year is a time of body detox, total rest and rejuvenation, alongside pockets of digital detox. Once a year I ensure I implement a full three nights of digital detox. It is usually close to the end of the year, but also try to build in regular pockets of two-day weekends of no screen time whatsoever. Whether #LocationFree or living life in general, I think that is an increasingly necessary habit to get into.

I also do one retreat a year where I am an active participant as opposed to the facilitator – be that a detox or yoga retreat, or something similar in which I do not have to think about anything other than the experience.

Being so far away from loved ones and family, it is vital to tune in to the holiday rhythms. I try to determine where I am going to be at significant times of the year, which is my way of staying connected, engaged, loved and loving. Knowing when and where I am going to see my partner, family, friends and clients also gives me a sense of being held and supported. For the first four years of being #LocationFree I was in a committed relationship, so I also built our together time into my year. I would go to South Africa at least three times every year, or he would come to my part of the world and we would travel together, and this rhythm was vital to keeping us connected. Luckily, intrinsic trust, respect and commitment were the values of our relationship. I always made sure that we spent our birthdays, Valentine's Day and other annual celebrations together. We didn't always get this right, mind you! But I also know that if I hadn't been paying attention to the bigger rhythm of the year, it would have been dire.

Establishing that rhythm ensured that I wasn't just gallivanting off around the world, ignoring the precious people who make up the matrix of my life. Everyone I have ever chatted to along the way, or interviewed for this book, who has managed to live the nomadic way successfully, has had to find the right way in order for them to feel plugged in to family and friendship circles that feed their souls.

I also had to dovetail my annual rhythm around the regular work commitments I had already booked. Or ones that I wanted to allow space for, whether I had the work clinched yet or not. And that meant factoring in where our writing retreats were going to take place, my Mastermind retreats, client work and keynote talks for conferences.

In the first two years of being #LocationFree I would make sure that I was in South Africa for the tail end of July, the full month of August and the start of September (spring in the south). This worked well because my partner's birthday was the end of July, and historically August is one of my busiest and most lucrative months. In South Africa, we celebrate Women's Day on a different date to the rest of the world. Here we commemorate the point in history when women marched on parliament for equal rights and that falls on 9 August. So that quarter of the calendar year was one of my busiest times of year, particularly when it came to acting as the keynote speaker at events celebrating women – both public and corporate gigs. Then September was always a great time of year for the de-cluttering side of my business. I loved inspiring audiences about spring cleaning your life – helping clients think about releasing, letting go, de-cluttering, getting ready to sell their homes and make space. Yes, S P A C E!

So, it is clear then that the rhythm you set for the year must take into account those elements that, together, make for a well-rounded, intentional and purposeful life. I believe it's vital to be able to make space, time and energy for yourself, your work, your heart, your significant relationships and friends. Plus, having a well-thought-out rhythm is much easier on your pocket, body and environment, because there is not as much back and forth, haphazardly crossing the world, clocking up a gazillion air miles.

 **WHAT OTHERS SAY ABOUT ...**

Rhythm and the seasons

I really do enjoy warm weather. I have been spending most of my time in warm places since travelling full time. However, I did spend this past December/January in Germany and it was a reminder of how much I don't like cold weather. And so I intend on being in somewhat warm weather, if not warm weather, from here on. I am currently in Porto Escondido, Mexico. I was in Medellin, Columbia, before this.

—*Gene Ellis*

I chase the sun and try to be out of South Africa in the winter months. I only like winter when I'm skiing but sadly I incurred a knee injury on the slopes, so those days have ended for me. I also like choosing locations that are not English speaking and offer a different culture and perspective to what I'm used to. I find that my productivity and learning are exponential in those environments. There are so many places to visit so I try to go to new locations as often as possible. Whenever I return to a place I've already been to, it's always because of the people.

—*Lynne Scullard*

Following work does to a certain degree dictate where we go, but we're "go with the flow" type of people. Things in our life fall into place, and we don't usually have a plan. Pretty much everywhere we've been since making the decision to leave Canada has simply just come to us. I wouldn't have it any other way; I haven't hated one minute of this lifestyle.

Depending on where you are going in the world, you might want to look into what the weather is like. We were using compression sacks for our clothing, but our clothes outgrew them. You can't control the weather - you just buy more clothing if you need to.

As we both also really enjoy cooking, there is a certain quality of kitchen equipment that we prefer to use. We travel with what we call our nomadic kitchen, or the kitchen kit. We've been to houses that don't have a single sharp knife; they might look the part, but they're lying to you. So we have a kit that adds a bit of extra kilograms of weight, so that in order to make a beautiful healthy meal, we have the right tools.

As we have everything we need and love with us, we don't usually go shopping unless we need more clothing due to weather. Once in a while we might buy a bottle of wine or a bottle of nice alcohol, and other than that it's food we spend our money on.

—**Chris de Cap**

Because I was staying one year in South-East Asia and six months in Central America, climate was of lesser importance. I like warm weather. If I'd have to travel to places that have cold winters, I'd plan to stay between spring and autumn.

—**André Gussekloo**

I like to be away from NYC during the winter. That's the primary decision point. And then, depends on when Unsettled trips are to locations I'd like *to go or when I have friends travelling.*

—Uday Jhunjhunwala

Some locations I found, but some sort of found me. So rule #1 for me is to be open to what comes on my path. Besides that, I look for places where I can make a difference. For instance, with housesitting, I am very good with dogs, so I tend to find places with difficult dogs/pack, whether they need medication, have behavioural difficulties, are huge in size or numbers (my max so far has been 16 dogs in one household, as well as some domestic birds and some turtles). I could also find places with one or two easy dogs, but there are plenty options for those home owners to find care for their animals, whereas in the harder cases, I am often the only option for these people to go on holiday while knowing their beloved animals are well cared for.

I don't really pick seasons, or locations based on seasons. I love the sun, but I can also be very happy in a rainy Ireland, for example.

—Martin van den Berg

I am a sun-chaser by heart! Warm water, mountains, friendly people and lots of fruits and vegetables are my favourite ingredients for a place I want to stay for a while.

—Mette Glargaard

I have chosen my home bases based on my child's needs. If I didn't have to think of him, I would go wherever the sun shines, but avoiding peak seasons.

—Katia Enbuske

Okay, so I haven't chosen, I have accepted contracts, which have taken me to various parts of the world.

—Deborah Louise Botha

I prefer summer time, not too hot, neither cold.

—Nabila Welk

I don't want to be in winter any more. That's a reason for me to choose locations!

For men, the wardrobe is maybe easier. I have a suitcase of 30 kilograms and I don't buy new clothes. That's impossible.

—Jan van Kuijk

I follow the work, not the weather – winter is my preferred season, although I've had a perpetual summer for three years because of work demands. I have one main suitcase that is generally only 18 kilograms for summer and sometimes 21 kilograms for winter – I have a small change over of one to three winter pieces I leave at my eldest daughter's house, although I try to keep the 18 kilograms at all times …

I'm not a shopper or a good tourist so that suits me fine, and if I really want to buy something to commemorate a country or an occasion, I'll make sure I buy something useful like a replacement for something that is wearing out or a useful work item like a new pencil case or talking piece …

I think travel insurance is important and I make sure our organisation's travel insurance is always up to date.

I think it's partly why I tend to stay in motels more than with other people because beds in hotels have to have standards. And I know you can get some really bad ones in hotels as well, but usually you can kind of figure out by their star rating or something the quality of what it will be like. So I tend to stay in motels more with work anyway. But if I'm staying with other people, whether they're friends, family or strangers I've just met, I just kind of have to make the best of it.

—Dee Brooks

 **TOP TIPS!**

- Remember to tune back into the subtle rhythm of your year.
- Try out new concepts – it's often easier to embrace new ideas away from home.
- Build breathing techniques into your routine – this is the fastest way to reconnect with yourself and your spirit.

Wardrobe woes

WHILE YOU MAY THINK THIS chapter is just for the gals – no, no, no! This is about how on earth you manage your wardrobe and clothing, still look great, travel well, feel fabulous and be able to both work and live #LocationFree.

Wardrobe is an important aspect to consider when thinking about this way of living. When I first made that decision back in that November of 2015, one of the first places my eyes turned to in my cosy little treehouse was my wardrobe. Because of my ability to live (and teach about being) clutter free, I already had an ingrained minimalist wardrobe. Every item of clothing I owned fitted in an open-plan wardrobe. My apartment had an industrial feel, and my wardrobe was like an art installation.

My hanging space comprised a stainless-steel rod suspended by means of metal chain from the ceiling, and of course all my hangers were the same colour and faced the same way – a simple but effective de-cluttering trick so that the space looks more streamlined as opposed to higgledy-piggledy hangers of every size and colour. My shoes were all laid out neatly under the hanging clothes, just as you might find in a high-end boutique. I had one of those gorgeous modern minimalist bookshelves that lean against the wall – and I used that for my folding clothes.

To compartmentalise, I also placed some small, painted wooden storage containers for intimate smalls. Much easier and neater to toss knickers, socks and yoga gear into one of three small containers. I even had my sexiest pair of highest heels displayed on the top shelf of that bookcase, for a sassy vintage shop feel. I *loved* my wardrobe. To me, it was a marvel that made me smile every day. I also had a storage box with a bespoke lid for all my hair-styling equipment, ready to rock-'n-roll my hair. I know one day I will try to emulate a similar look in a permanent home! As part of my de-cluttering and minimalist philosophy, I live and teach the following code: You should love every single thing you own and it should add energy to your life. The specific questions I ask are:

- Do I *love* it?
- Do I *use* it?
- Does it add *energy* to my life?

If you can't answer *Yes!* to all three, then it – whatever it is – has no place in your life. When I was about to embark on my new #LocationFree life, I had to add the extra wardrobe question: Will this be travelling in my suitcase? If not, – it needed a new home, pronto!

So, even with my pared-down wardrobe, I still had too much clothing that wasn't practical for travelling and living #LocationFree. I was ruthless. I invited my assistant over and gifted a fifth of my wardrobe to her. Some of it went to a charity shop, or was passed on to others, and the rest I was able to keep and take with me. I even found a new home for my precious

Harley Davidson denim jacket from the days when I owned a Harley. Yes I really did own a bike!

By then I already understood the concept now known as a "capsule wardrobe", in which you have everything you need to create multiple "looks". Everything is bought with the purpose of mixing and matching and co-ordinating with flexibility, usually with some thread of a colour scheme or a vibe or theme that ties it all together. A lot of people only understand the importance of this when, for example, they are going on an island holiday. Perhaps you choose royal blue as your main colour and then everything you buy slots into that "holiday colour" vibe.

About to embark on my #LocationFree adventure, however, I now needed to take this to a whole new level, because your *entire* wardrobe needs to work together in a similar way. And be light. And easy to wash. There is little point of having items that can only be worn in one way – unless, of course, it's that sassy little black number for gals or that well-cut jacket for guys when you need to glam up a little.

Remember, though, that #LocationFree is not akin to backpacking like students – your wardrobe has to be small and multifunctional, super practical and super light in weight.

I had for many years lived according to the principle of less is more. I tried to buy quality staples that cost a fair amount – think tailored black trousers, a perfectly cut crease-free jacket and a pair of incredible heels that go with pretty much everything. Then, annually, I would layer on top of that trendy, cheaper, fashionable items. Those tend to have a shorter life span than the quality staples and you may only wear them for one or two seasons.

Because of the practicality of a smaller travelling wardrobe, you tend to wear stuff out a lot quicker, and get bored of it sooner because you are literally wearing and washing it far more often than when living in a fixed place where you have a lot to choose from every day. You might only wear a shirt three or four times in a regular season at home, but when travelling that might be upped to twice a week! It's a great lesson in staying less attached to items of clothing. You might also choose to only have one handbag, purse, backpack or computer bag. Yes, it means less of a choice, but also that you absolutely *love* every item you keep 10 times more. And be willing to part with it sooner!

It also helps to think about multipurpose clothing that can be worn in a variety of ways, as well as interchangeable mix-and-match options, and clothing from fabric that travels well (remember, though, that synthetic fibres aren't good for menopausal hot flashes) or is super easy to wash and dry. Definitely no "dry cleaning only" items. Can you image how much time, money and energy that would require?

Unless I was going to be wearing something a few times a week, every week, I couldn't really justify space for it in my suitcase. So, apart from my salsa dancing shoes, which stayed packed up in one of my three forever boxes, the rule was: if it didn't come *with me*, it was no longer part of my wardrobe. (And in case you're wondering, I still managed to dance, just in regular shoes!)

I also pretty much made up my mind that the general rhythm of my year would not include travelling to the far north or to countries in the throes of hellish winter. Having said that, I did land up once in the UK for three months of winter. The simple solution was to borrow from my mum, and to add *layers* – and lots of them – just to look like the Michelin Man.

My wardrobe needed to be more suitable for summer, and what travel agents call the "shoulder seasons" of spring and autumn. I fell in love with pashminas and scarves, which are super small, lightweight, easy to pack and can improve or update or change up most outfits. They are also great for travelling on planes because they double up as a pillow or a light covering in an airport chair. Just three of those in different colours in a capsule wardrobe can add umpteen different looks and possibilities. I remember in particular one of the most heart-warming compliments I ever received, when someone noticed how small my wardrobe was, and couldn't believe it because I was always "so impeccably dressed" and never seemed to wear the same thing twice. Well, well, well …

So, what is your wardrobe challenge? My advice is to get some help! Having worked with awesome wardrobe stylists and image consultants over the years, particularly for events I was involved in, I fully understood the concept of "styling" a look. A capsule wardrobe is simply about taking that to the next level. Drag your clever, stylish and know-it-all clothing friend along with you through a tour of your wardrobe or hire a professional stylist or wardrobe consultant to give you some pointers or take you shopping. I promise, it's money well spent!

The exercise will also teach you how to dress for your body shape and colouring, and to think about clothes differently, which in turn will make it easier for you when replacing stuff – the better you know the rules, the easier to follow them and know when to break them!

People always ask: What about shoes? I generally have six pairs and travel with the following combo: one pair of all-trail shoes, one pair super-comfy all-day walking trainers, one pair casual Converse, one pair sassy flat sandals, one pair flip-flops and one pair of super-sexy high heels. I can pretty much cover any outfit and every function with that combination! And, to help lessen my baggage weight, I always travel on long-haul flights wearing the heaviest, of course. All my shoes mix and match with everything else. You can definitely get away with less, but that for me is more of a holiday vibe, not a permanent on-the-road lifestyle.

The one-in-one-out rule

One of the amazing benefits to being #LocationFree is that you get to be in different counties and be exposed to so many beautiful items. Everyone has his or her own little "rules" for this. I remember when, in my twenties, I backpacked around South East Asia for three months on my own, and my little rule was that I was allowed *one* item from each country. So, if I saw something that I loved on the first day, and bought it immediately, then that was that. Simple. The rest had to be a feast of the eyes, not the purse. As a child, I had learned to love window-shopping, so I can be inspired, moved and fulfilled by spotting something without it necessarily having to come home with me. In this more recent phase of living #LocationFree, I allow myself to buy along the way, but usually when something else needs replacing. For instance, on one trip to Greece I suddenly realised that I was sick and tired of a gorgeous red dress. Now don't get me wrong ... The dress was still in tiptop shape, but I just couldn't bear to wear it one more time. I had purchased it for a Valentine's couples' retreat for the YPO and had worn it for many keynote talks, and I had just had enough of it. Bye-bye!

Knowing that its time had come, I summoned my landlady up to my flat above her home – she would look like a goddess in it! I made her try it on and she, beaming, looked just fabulous. My heart was thus happy as that dress had a new home and, of course, I now had space and reason to go and buy one more little dress – a luscious lemon-yellow Greek linen dress that I still have.

With all of that said, however, when you have a visible brand and a business that keeps you in the public eye, you can't be seen to be wearing the same signature piece too often or for every single talk on stage. It's just not professional and I was once told that by people who care!

Firstly, my PR said, "Kate, we need a new set of brand pictures of you soon, because I just can't send these ones out any more. As much as they are great and en point, all the media have already seen them over and over again!" I also learned that for professional brand pics, you should ideally update them every two years! Perhaps this is more specific to women because we can change our hair, glasses and overall look a little more often than guys, right? And perhaps age a little differently too. Secondly, my personal stylist friend, who had her own range of ready-to-wear clothing line, said, "Kate, I just can't any more ... If I see one more pic of you in that damn jacket I'm going to die." Ouch – and it was even her clothing range!

So, apart from the one-out-one-in rule – one that I impose on myself not without some flexibility – another trick is that every time I am packing to leave a location I have been at for about three months, I use the opportunity to re-evaluate by asking myself three more questions:

- Do I still love it?
- Can I still use or wear it?
- Does it still add energy to my life?

I might then choose to let go of a few items and make space for gifts in my suitcase, especially if I have been travelling to loved ones for birthdays or Christmas.

Jewellery

Guys and gals are perhaps different when it comes to jewellery – generally speaking, anyway, so please don't shoot the messenger ... Guys tend to wear a minimum, their watches possibly the exception. But for gals – and, again, this is purely from my experience and a generalisation, I know – jewellery is a *huge* part of dressing and accessorising. I am a little different in that I tend to be quite minimal (or lazy ...). I usually wear jewellery that generally stays on permanently, even when I sleep, shower or swim. I find it a pain to have to pull stuff on and off, so I wear a simple combo of earrings, rings, necklaces and bracelets. I have a bit of gypsy energy and love shiny silver baubles. I also have a few pieces I use to make an outfit pop, make a statement or that has some significant meaning for me: a pair of fancy black drop earrings for an elegant night out or a funky thread of multicoloured beads to add a sense of fun and change up my look a little. Remember the "altar" I discussed as part of my rituals in Lesson 5? I find that having four small tins or containers works well for me because they double up as jewellery boxes and sit proudly on my sacred altar. The tins themselves are important to me: precious gifts from loved ones that have become not only part of my packing, compartmentalising and travelling routine, but also mementoes that make me happy and feel connected to loved ones. One is a heart with *Love* written on it, gifted to me when I first started travelling; one a Day of the Dead skull shape for rings and earrings; one with a yellow Native American inlay design from my mum; another a wooden inlay fiftieth-birthday gift from Spain.

Now let's get packing ...

Long before Japanese organising guru Marie Kondo rose to fame, and decades before I started organising and de-cluttering as a profession, I had been packing a certain way when travelling. When I was seven, I went to boarding school and everything for the full three-month semester had to fit in a single black trunk. Then, at the age of eight, I took my first trip across South Africa to the mining town of Kuruman with German neighbours. My Nan showed me how to *roll* clothes, teaching me that you always manage to pack far more in a suitcase, and they wrinkle less along the way. And she was right! Thanks, Nan. Plus, when I was much older, she showed me, when travelling with linen or any fabric that tends to crease a lot, how to use tissue paper layered in between your clothes – and those you might lay flat on top of the rolled layer underneath.

I have since perfected a combination of "rolled and folded" developed over the years – I call it "rolded". This is also how I get most of my clients to pack when de-cluttering and organising homes, wardrobes and shelves. It's much easier to see and use stuff when it is in a vertical pile and you have visual access to it. Think about that big pile of T-shirts – and, of course, you always want to wear the one smack in the middle, don't ya? Then, as you try to delicately remove it, the whole pile topples over in a heap …

Having access to everything makes life so much easier. Think a favourite store that might have all their T-shirts rolled in a drawer. You open the drawer and can see all the colours of the same T-shirt laid out in front of you. Or perhaps it's a drawer of socks, or ties. When you pull one out, you don't mess up the entire drawer.

Don't you hate it when a store has those big piles and, once you've made your selection, the shop assistant materialises in two seconds flat to tidy that damn pile so that it looks neat and tidy again. Such an impractical pain in the butt, isn't it?

Now, when I open my suitcase, I can pretty much access everything I need. Remember when I first moved to my partner's house at the very beginning of this #LocationFree lifestyle and I lived out of my suitcase? Well, that's because it was perfectly packed and super easy to remove clothing in a flash, and repack clean washing in just a few seconds. With three quarters of the items rolded, my entire wardrobe is available at a glance.

Have you ever looked at one of those old-fashioned "travelling trunks", the kind you often see in the movies? Well, when I was three we emigrated from the UK to South Africa and some of our stuff was packed in those trunks and, for the first few years in our new home, I had one of those as my wardrobe. I loved it so much. You unlock and open the trunk and flip it upright, and it magically becomes a standing wardrobe. When you need to travel or move, you then simply close up the trunk and off you go. Genius and multipurpose from eons ago.

Toiletries

To be honest, after my shoes, toiletries make up the bulk of weight when travelling. One packing trick recommended by a lot of travellers is simply not to travel with any bulky toiletries at all and rather replace them in your next destination. That just doesn't work for me.

I do what I call a combo travel hack. I have smaller travel-sized containers to refill and, as I am about to leave, I make sure I finish the bulkier items such as shampoo, conditioner and shower gel, and then decant the small remaining amounts into the travel-sized containers. These generally last about a week, which gives me a few days to settle and then replace them without too much stress.

I also liked to travel with my preferred skincare products. I really do my utmost not to compromise on face products just because I live around the world. For a few years, when I was living permanently in South Africa, I was very lucky to be one of the local ambassadors for Dermalogica. From the moment I started using their incredible range, it became my product of choice and, seven years later, it still is. So, at a very practical level, I make sure I have what I need from Dermalogica for up to three months at a time. All of this is, of course, not only about the self-care component of taking care of my ageing skin, but also helps establish my own important routine.

All my toiletries and medicines are always beautifully compartmentalised. Remember my batching concept of "like with like"? It's the perfect packing tip and is what I teach in my book *Clear Your Clutter*: medicines with medicines, make-up with make-up, daily toiletries together, jewellery together – all in easy-to-find pouches, tins or packing cubes that are easy to pack on a shelf or in a drawer. No time or energy wasted on looking for what is needed.

To make life much easier, I have another very practical way of storing, packing and using everyday toiletries. The products I use twice a day are all organised and stand upright in a single white plastic organiser that contains all my facial products, body oil, deodorant, toothbrush and toothpaste, hair-styling products, hairbrush and perfume. That organiser is the first item I retrieve from my suitcase and I pop it on the bathroom shelf. It's always stacked the same way, which makes it easy to see any item I need. The idea is to be able to emulate your own bathroom at home where you always know where your toothbrush is.

I don't like travelling cosmetic bags that unfold and hang; they are not practical for me. I could never be bothered to dig around in a pouch or rifle through items rolling loose around inside my suitcase. Everything must fit neatly into that white, lightweight storage container – all modern bathroom stores or "organising" shops stock similar items nowadays – and when packing up, I pop the entire container and contents into a waterproof drawstring bag to prevent leakage onto clothes. At the next destination, in two seconds flat, I can remove it and pop it on the washbasin or bathroom shelf.

You get the logic, right? It not only saves time and energy, but also helps establish a routine or habit whereby I never have to think, "Mmm … now where's my perfume?" Packing tricks are all about efficiency for me, not wasting one a nanosecond or energy looking, because everything is always where it needs to be.

Medicines

All my travelling medicines are in one small pouch. I generally carry small amounts of everyday meds, homeopathic tinctures and essential oils, along with an antibiotic cream, plasters and disinfectant swabs. All in *one* small see-through cosmetic bag. I always take everything out of their boxes because those just waste space!

Make-up

Everything I own and use fits into one small-ish zipped make-up bag. To be honest, it is probably the size most women pop in their huge handbag or purse. I live fastidiously according to the philosophy of less is more. Many years ago a friend who is a professional make-up artist taught me how to apply make-up not only so that I can dash out the door and still look polished (two-in-one powder, top-lash mascara and a slick of lip gloss in 20 seconds flat), but also every-day make-up and then how to ramp it up for night-time glam. It was a magic morning well spent. I have since mastered the art of being able to create a more dramatic look when attending a fancy event or speaking on stage. I now carry the following with me:

- 1 x light foundation with SPF
- 1 x concealer stick for pesky blemishes
- 2 x mascaras (black, of course, and a beach girl needs royal blue too)
- 2 x eyeliners that can also be worn on top of each other (one chocolate brown and the second a gorgeous glitter glam)
- 1 x multipurpose highlighter blush and brush
- 1 x tinted eyebrow "gel" for impact if I haven't had eyebrows professionally groomed
- 1 x small multicoloured eye-shadow kit for a bit of ooh-la-la.
- 3 x lipsticks (pink, red and nude)
- 4 x lip glosses (I have them in every bag, purse or pocket – best present you can ever give me.)
- 1 x pair tweezers
- 1 x nail file
- 1 x small heart-shaped mirror compact.

And that's *it*! Nothing more.

Most women have *far* too much make-up that they never use. And it goes rancid. My rule is to keep the volume small, love it, use it, kill it and replace it.

Guys, of course, tend to have it a whole lot easier … All they generally need are a handful of grooming items for shaving, nail and hair care.

 **WHAT OTHERS SAY ABOUT ...**

Packing for travel

I travel super light. Most people don't believe me, but on my last trip to South America I travelled with only a cabin bag, a vanity bag, and a regular backpack. That was for two and a half months. I don't check in luggage. I always check in online and download my boarding pass so I can go straight through security and customs.

I pack mix-and-match items and keep it simple. I include a light linen jacket for smarter occasions, lightweight clothing and shoes. I roll my clothes so that they don't crease much and also so that I can fit more into my bag. My packing is very intentional, and spatial awareness goes a long way when knowing what to fit into what.

I am not a big shopper at all so I rather invest my time and money on experiences that add meaning and joy to my life – in other words, on memorable occasions that embed great "forever memories". If I happen to pass by something that I really like, and the chance of me getting it anywhere else is slim, then I may enter the shop and buy it. If it's heavy or bulky I don't even consider it.

—Lynne Scullard

Packing, I must say, still stresses me. The one thing that I struggle with is what happens if my luggage goes missing (which it has done). So I always have two bags and cross pack into both of those. This just safeguards you. I have recently had a situation where both suitcases never arrived, so you need to have a back-up plan for your back-up plan. (PS. I never had this.)

Another practical tip is to wear layers when travelling. You can never predict what you will find if you are in transit and going from one climate to another. I always make sure I am wearing stretchy, comfortable clothes as you don't want to be sitting in tight jeans (well, not for a 16-hour flight).

I also make sure I wear comfortable pop-off sneakers, so that I can allow my feet the reality of swelling on a plane, but also know that if I need to walk from one transit lounge or terminal to another, that I am comfortable and prepared. If you are prone to swelling in your feet and legs, I strongly recommend pressure socks – they really do work.

I have an Amazon account, and have found the online space and shopping particularly useful and convenient. I believe once we see what our new normal is, after Covid19, this will be even more relevant and widely used as a shopping platform.

—Deborah Louise Botha

All my clothes can be combined, from very casual to sophisticated. Just one suitcase, and one bag for my MacBook, iPad and phone.

I love good, healthy food and buy local, so that's never a problem. Personal care can be a bit complicated in some areas, but knowing that, I might take a second bottle of my favourite shampoo with me. Up to now, I never had a problem to get what I really like.

—Nabila Welk

Roll up all your clothes!

I will only get clothes or computer accessories. Bigger or less essential items will have to wait until I settle down again. I will usually buy in physical shops, because varying shipping times would force me to stay in one location for a longer period.

—André Gussekloo

I do not bring anything more than a carry-on suitcase. That is all that I have. It allows me to avoid paying for luggage charges and just really forces you to focus on the things you need. I do a fold-and-roll packing technique so you can actually fit quite a lot of clothing into a carry-on suitcase, definitely a couple weeks' worth of clothing. If it doesn't fit in the carry-on then it doesn't get purchased. That's my rule. I will not get a bigger suitcase and I will not get a storage unit. Either it fits in the luggage or it doesn't get purchased.

—Gene Ellis

For the most part, I try to travel with carry-on except if I'm spending a lot of time in one place and not travelling much. Also, it depends on having access to laundry.

—Uday Jhunjhunwala

I pack as light as possible, not to have the lightest pack as possible, but to be able to comfortably bring the few luxury items that really make me happy during my stay, like my iPad or my hammock. This was especially the case during my two years of travelling with just a backpack, a little less so now that I often travel with my campervan.

Another tip is to make sure you know what situation you are going to. For instance, I once went to a housesit in Bulgaria, where I arrived with all my 300 books on my iPad, only to discover the house had no electricity or running water (and not a book in the house). Had I known this beforehand, I would have brought paper books, of course.

In regard to wardrobe, I always think in layers. So if I bring two sweaters in wintertime, I will try to have different ones in terms of size and insulation value, so one can go over the other if needed and combine into a third option.

Practise non-attachment. Period. Inner happiness is lasting happiness, while the happiness found in "things" like your favourite chocolate, coffee or peanut butter is a fleeting one. Any search engine can help you translate labels in the supermarket in case you really need to stick to a gluten-free diet or something, and/or prepare a local vegetable. And if not, it is an excellent excuse to introduce yourself to your neighbours and ask for tips.

—Martin van den Berg

I pack as little as possible. It gives me an opportunity to support the local economy and wear something that is fit for the place I am in. I do, however, carry great hiking shoes, since I love hiking. Every country has everything you need, so underwear is the only thing I am picky about and buy certain brands. I order online and normally find a resort or similar that can be the recipient for my orders.

—Mette Glargaard

I have a pretty minimalist wardrobe that was designed as a uniform but when I got to Spain, it didn't work. I had zero smart summer clothes! I had to buy a few items when I got to Malaga and I had to look at my style differently. Black isn't a colour to be worn in the summer!

Shopping ... I buy quality and never more than I need. I'm a sucker for stationery, though. I'm sure I could fill a suitcase with journals ... oops!

—Carolynne Alexander

So this only came to me recently because it's been a learning of how am I going to live with only the stuff in my suitcase? And I'm really excited with how I'm doing it at the moment. So I have created what I call a wardrobe swap. If I buy something, I lose something. Generally, when I'm packing, I will actually purposefully put in some stuff that I'm prepared to ditch along the way so that when I accumulate something new, I am very comfortable to donate what I just am parting with. And I am now completely buying from second-hand stores, of which there is an enormous offering in Latin America and Europe. There are so many good quality second-hand stores so I only shop from them. I've limited my colour scheme now – only have a handful of colours that become part of the wardrobe. I've only just settled on one combination at the moment so I may in time decide on others. The luggage is the really interesting thing I want to challenge myself with. I learned from my recent trip to Europe for 60 days travelling across 16 different countries, that you could buy super cheap and cheerful air tickets. They become less cheap and cheerful the minute you've got to put your luggage in the hold. So I do want to try to bring myself down to a carry-on for a longer-term period of travel. That's my challenge this year. Which might mean more of the wardrobe rotation.

—**Michelle Clarke**

When travelling between countries or somewhere else I only travel with my handbag and a light Ikea sports bag that weighs almost nothing. So, I can pack it full of clothes and my laptop travels in my handbag. I've been on the road for three weeks like this and with this gear I could go on for three months if I wanted. I have a selection of clothes that are light, easy to wash, fast to dry, don't wrinkle and outfits can be matched in many ways. I always have one nicer dress for fancier occasions, but also light and non-wrinkling material. I always pack my lightweight duvet jacket, gloves and a warm cap and a hat against sun, flip-flops for the beach, hot weather and cold floors and a light sarong I can use as towel, dress, beach towel, blanket, cover for head etcetera. If I'm on the road I don't shop much, because shopping means getting rid of something else. I only buy what I need. I have travelling insurance from my country, which is valid for three months at a time. If I'm away longer I can buy extra days in my insurance.

—**Katia Enbuske**

We had six months to de-clutter, selling, donating, or just giving away most of our possessions as everything we now own fits into a large car. I severely reduced my wardrobe, just keeping a few items of clothing to suit each season. I did have to part with many favourite dresses and shoes. We have one large suitcase and one cabin-sized, then all other clothes fit into packing cubes (as these can be crammed into small spaces in the car) and vacuum bags. I didn't consider that most Southern European houses don't have vacuum cleaners, so have to suck the air out myself until I'm light-headed – the reverse of blowing up a balloon!

We bought travel cages for our African Grey parrot. Three in total as I had to return the first two as they didn't fit into the car. The parrot goes in the middle of the back seat, with a dog either side. We also have the biggest roof box the store could supply and a dog barrier to stop items in the back sliding forward on top of the pets. It happened …

We live and eat like locals, so purchase most things in the town wherever we are. Not having a permanent address makes it very difficult to order online so, on occasion, we've paid for a PO Box at the nearest post office. Other times, items are sent to family in the UK, then they either bring them when they visit, or we pick up when we return to England on visits.

Rob plays Tetrus with our belongings each time we move and the car is literally bursting at the seams. I usually end up with bags on my feet and knees and there's always a bag of dirty laundry on top of Woody's cage! Therefore, we cannot buy new stuff – if it doesn't fit in the car, we have to leave it behind and we've deliberately, and accidently done so with some items.

—Nancy Benn

 **WHAT OTHERS SAY ABOUT ...**

Travel insurance

In terms of travel insurance, I think it's very important. I had a friend end up US$70,000 in debt because he got into a motorbike accident in Thailand. Although Thailand is a relatively cheap country, there are certainly scenarios that can be very expensive. His quality of care suffered because he didn't have insurance and he really needed to be treated back in the USA, but the medical flight was about $30 000. A $40-a-month insurance policy would have paid for that. So I definitely suggest travel insurance. At the bare minimum, you should have travel insurance for emergencies, but really you should have international health insurance because for a lot of travel insurances, if your injuries are very, very bad, they will just ship you back to your home country. If you don't have insurance there, you're just in a really bad situation. I know that in certain countries it's not a big problem because they have free healthcare, but in some places like the USA, it's better to have an international health plan like Cigna Global, Bupa, and things like that.

—Gene Ellis

I have always looked at travel insurance as a nice-to-have but not crucial. I have now changed my mind and I believe we really should not travel without it. In my line of business and watching what the tourism and travel industry is currently facing with the recent global health situation, the people who have been hardest hit and left stranded are the ones who didn't take out the travel insurance.

I think we really need to consider the question, "What if?" I believe when you look at what can go wrong, when travelling and living/working abroad, you cannot be without some sort of safety net in the form of travel insurance. The worst might not happen, but if it does, you want to know that you are covered.

—Deborah Louise Botha

As we were travelling for more than 30 days, mainstream travel- and car-insurance policies would not provide cover; therefore, I had to undertake some extensive research during the six months before departing to find annual car and health insurance to protect us for unlimited travel in Europe. The main issue was not having a permanent address in Europe, as many providers were not prepared to use our UK address when we were obviously not living there.

—Nancy Benn

I usually book my tickets with a credit card that gives you free travel insurance and I have a local medical aid that covers you for 90 days at a time out of South Africa. When I know I'll be engaging in high-risk sports such as skiing, I always take top-up insurance.

—Lynne Scullard

Do get one! And hold on to all your receipts, boarding passes, transport tickets, ATM receipts ...

—André Gussekloo

I get an annual coverage from Allianz. I've been very happy with them.

—Uday Jhunjhunwala

Absolutely necessary! I have bank N26 and they give me travel insurance for 15 euro a month.

—Mette Glargaard

 **TOP TIPS!**

- Get help building a clever "capsule wardrobe" for your specific lifestyle.
- Remember that you really *can* buy most things along the way.
- Once your suitcase is packed, go back and take out another third. You just won't need it!

The LAY Principle: Look After Yourself

IN THIS CHAPTER I DELVE into one of the most important factors of being on the road. The LAY Principle is all about how to Look After Yourself.

I am super lucky to be able to say that, apart from niggling back issues and some aches and pains, I have been sick only once while abroad – throwing up in a client's home in Lagos in the middle of a workshop. That was a low point. I had to run out of the circle, find the bathroom, throw up and then wash my face, walk back into the room and promptly carry on working as if nothing had happened – even though they all heard me through the thin walls. Cringe. I also tested positive for Covid19 in March 2020 when travelling from South Africa to the UK to be with my mum for lockdown. I was extremely fortunate in that I experienced quite mild symptoms, the hardest hit being my chest (probably due to my history of asthma), and went straight into isolation for three weeks before I was confident enough to dare risk contact with my mum. Other than that little scare amid a worldwide pandemic, I have learned how best to take care of myself living this kind of lifestyle.

I believe you have to be especially vigilant and make self-care a priority! I think the lesson look after oneself when travelling was instilled in me many decades ago. I was 22 years old and, after working in the UK for a year, I went gallivanting by myself as a single young female. I headed solo though South East Asia. I must have been part mad, part stubborn, courageous and a combo of many attributes. I had never met anyone else who had travelled through that area and there were even jihads (holy wars) all though the region. This was well before the days of mobile phones, travel wallets, online access and social media. My itinerary was largely nonexistent. I had booked a flight from London to Katmandu with *no* hotel confirmed even for the first night. Two weeks later I took a flight from Nepal to Bangkok, and finally two and a half months after that to the Southern Indonesian island of Timor to fly into Darwin. Three months of exploring, solo. I had already secured a two-year work visa for Australia and New Zealand, and had about 25 friends from my travels waiting for me – to host me, offer me work, etcetera.

Picture this ... I get off the plane in the searing heat of Katmandu, and am instantly bombarded with everything hot, humid, odorous: cows, throngs of people, masses of shouting. Somehow, I manage to catch a local tuk-tuk into the centre and, using the paperback edition of *The Lonely Planet* travel guide, proceed to follow the maps to areas where I believe there are low-cost hostels. En route – I kid you not because the image is forever etched in my mind – I turn a corner on the cobbled street and am looking up, admiring the kaleidoscope of colours on the fluttering prayer flags, the incense, the smoke, the smells, just in total awe of all that was in front of my eyes. As I adjust my backpack to even out the weight, I look back down at the street to check where I am heading. Just ahead on my left I spot a small gathering. As I get closer, I see to my horror a dead cow lying in the road. The "butcher" is standing over the cow, carving out lumps of meat. There are flies buzzing and dogs drooling everywhere. The stench is overpowering. He is cutting (uhm … hacking) chunks of varying sizes to order, wrapping the meat in paper, filthy notes shoved into his bloody hands, and off the happy customer prances.

At the time I was an avid meat eater, and growing up in South Africa I had long been a huge fan of something we call biltong (a little like what Americans call jerky, but way better), a devoted carnivore. I also did not have an appetite for anything too spicy – I didn't even like chutney (Mrs Balls in South Africa was even too hot for me) or too much pepper. I was a curry lightweight, through and through.

My whole body recoiled in disgust and horror at the scene in front of me – cow hide split open, belly, ribs and innards exposed to the direct sun, flies stuck in the meat, and the stench of flesh that must surely already be rotting. I made a split decision: *If I eat meat I'm going to die!*

And that was it … I was an instant vegetarian and that night I went out and ordered the most delicious lentil curry. *Curry?* I went from carnivore and chilli novice to vegetarian gourmet who laced every meal with some form of chilli, cumin, coriander, red chilli, and green chilli, you name it. Up until that point in my life, I had also been bulimic (a journey I share in *Ditch Your Glitch*) and had been carrying a lot of excess weight. Body baggage. Unlike anorexia, bulimics can be any size and weight and generally have that unhealthy dull, bloated look about them. Yep, that was me.

I also had what we used to call a "bum bag", or "fanny pack" in which I carried *all my money* in traveller's cheques (not one credit card in sight) for the full three months of my trip, along with my cash on hand. I knew how much I could spend each day and each week. Nothing was prepaid so I was carrying my entire life, including my passport and ID, on my person. The type of accommodation I stayed in meant it was safer to carry that stuff *with* me at all times.

At the same time that I made the split decision to not eat meat, I also decided I had better go really easy on the alcohol, so that I could keep my wits about me.

At the end of the day, it was about survival. I remember one day in those three months, when I was on a smaller island off Lombok (to the east of Bali) in a very safe area and witnessed the fishermen bring the fish off the boat straight to the home I was staying in. That night I ate fresh fish and had a glass of wine. Heaven! But it was a once off. I remained mostly vegetarian (eating only eggs and dairy) for the next five years, until my body asked for animal protein again. The point of sharing this story is that my decisions were all about self-care and self-preservation. What do you need to do to look after yourself when you are on the road?

A few decades on, with some minor health issues in my medical history, I had to remember to keep the LAY principle uppermost in my mind. I have already shared my feelings about the beds I sleep in and needing to be cognisant of my lower-back injury (*see* Settling In in Lesson 3). Living #LocationFree is not about slumming it, nor about only staying in posh five-star hotels. It is about the day-to-day, month-to-month way of looking after my business, my life and my body. #LocationFree removed any semblance of a routine you might otherwise follow, or having the comfort of a neighbourhood that you know intimately. You have to learn to rely on yourself that much more, especially if you are not in one community for too long, building up that network of support.

You have to understand your body and what it needs to stay healthy and energised. It's different for everyone, of course, but you have to keep self-care at the top of your list because travelling and living #LocationFree requires a different kind of alertness, of energy and ability to stay tuned in. #LocationFree tests your resilience – of body, mind/heart and spirit.

Body

Travelling takes its toll, irrespective of how glamorous anyone makes it look. (For further information on travel insurance, *see* the discussion in Lesson 4.) When I was moving across time zones, between South Africa and the USA, my body really battled to adjust and integrate. I used to travel with melatonin pills to help my internal rhythm adjust quicker to the new time zone. It wasn't available in some countries, so I always made sure I had a little stash to last just three days.

With my personal history of back issues and a couple of slipped discs, I remember my chiropractor not only telling me about how different beds can wreak the havoc, but also how the actual travelling is just as hard on your body. Not only sitting upright in awfully small seats for endless hours – some trips were 16-hour flights – but also the simple logistics of travelling: climbing in and out of buses, taxis, cars, trains, buses and planes at airports. (I only ever flew Business Class a few times, but at least that helped me enjoy being able to lie flat and quaff Champagne.) Add to this is the actual cabin pressure, along with recycled cabin air and what that does to your body.

Although I have always been far more inclined to use homeopathic, aromatherapy and naturopathic remedies, I still kept a small cocktail of pain medication at hand. I had been prescribed it for three months when bed ridden for my injured back, and my awesome chiropractor suggested that, with my extensive travel, I keep a very small amount of all three for an emergency should the travelling "tweak" anything. His initial intervention had meant that I was able to avoid a back operation, so I trusted his advice implicitly. The cocktail was meant to break the pain cycle. As much as I resisted, I also knew that one blast (a muscle relaxant, pain killer and anti-inflammatory) was like a big fat fluffy hug from the world of comfort. So I learned to trust that I needed them at hand for just in case. I kept all together in one tin, and hardly ever had to pull those babies out. I still travel with them to this day!

My go-to, of course, has always been alternative options. For instance, my mum found an incredible natural joint ointment, called Joint Ace, in the UK. What a little tube of magic! It is always in my suitcase. She brings me two tubes whenever we see each other. It is way better than arnica oil for me and its gooey texture makes it better for travelling, because it is less likely to leak. It is a natural combination of chondoitrin, glucosamine and aromatherapy oils, and remains my saving grace. I also carry homeopathic arnica, Rescue Remedy and lavender essential oil.

Next up in maintaining your body is exercise ... I follow simple routines that can be done in most places: walk, yoga, swim and cycle! As mentioned in Lesson 5 (The Zap of Zen), I have always been into yoga and have been practising it in some form or other since I was a teenager. Granted, I go through phases, but it always calls me back. As smart phone apps improved, I investigated those options and now use the Down Dog app to guide me through a practice. A number of hotels have gyms, but that's not really my scene and I would much rather do the yoga in my bedroom, and then take a walk to explore. If there's a pool, I swim daily.

I always do my best to find a local yoga studio; many studios have great first-time offers. I then do my best to practise every day – plus, for me it's always a great way to start connecting into the community. It also allows me to get out of the apartment or house. I have also started attending yoga retreats as part of my annual schedule, knowing that those breaks are life sustaining. My first choice whenever I'm in a new city is to walk. There's nothing like it. And all I need is a combination of good shoes, comfortable socks, a cross-body handbag or small backpack, and some water in order to explore.

My second choice is to rent a bicycle, and sometimes a housesitting job offers access to a bicycle. Usually when looking after dogs, walking them daily is part of the energy exchange. I would try to alternate looking after dogs with cats to enjoy different routines. Once I looked after three dogs that couldn't be walked at the same time, which meant I had to do two different walks every day, in a hilly area in the hills of San Francisco! Did I get fit? Hell, yeah!

Sleep is also vital for self-care. I am an early bird by nature, so prefer to be in bed and sleeping my 10 pm and up with the sun at 6 am. That's my natural rhythm, and it keeps my energy aligned and healthy. I know more self-care is needed whenever I start going to bed too late because I'm watching too many movies or Netflix series on my laptop. It's fine for the most part, but it can take escapism too far and then messes with my body. I would then try to go into self-observation mode: "Ah, Kate, look at you – you must be processing and ignoring something else going on." Watching that screen in bed is completely addictive, so I would let myself revel in it for a maximum of two weeks, and then force myself back into reading at night before I drift off to sleep.

At the end of the day, we have to know how to be self-aware, no matter what. To be able to laugh at ourselves and gently pull ourselves back into more nourishing habits, those that nurture us.

Part of what falls under the heading of Look After Yourself is looking after my appearance. That includes hair, nails and skin, for example. I have had short funky hair with a pop of colour for over 11 years. One of the hardest things is finding a hairdresser who thinks like I do. The same goes for nails – I was a habitual nail biter since a child, and when my speaking career took off, I knew I had to find a way to up my game when it came to personal grooming.

I like to have my nails painted with gel or shellac. That keeps me groomed, makes me take better care of my hands, and prevents me from biting my nails when I'm stressed. But some habits die hard, don't they? So when I land in a new place, and I am there for more than two weeks, it's a priority to find a nail salon. My hair also needs cutting at least every five to six weeks, or it looks like a giant pouffe; my hair grows fast and gets big and bouncy. It also instantly ages me. Ugh. The same goes for eyebrows.

I guess all these things are so simple when you're living in one place; you simply call for an appointment or pop into your favourite spot. There is zero thinking or stress around it. Living #LocationFree, however, I had to manage this properly in order to feel that I was taking care of my appearance and self-care routine. As mentioned, I use Dermalogica skin care, which is awesome for travelling because products last three months. Every time I stock up, I get the few things I need all at once, knowing I am good to go for another few months. I also try local organic products along the way. It's a great way to support the local community and country you are in, and have found some new favourites, especially Greek products!

Body work is another aspect of self-care I keep high on my radar. Depending on the country I am visiting, I tap into what is local and delicious. For instance, when visiting Lesvos in Greece for our annual writing retreats, I head for the ancient thermal hot springs. My body demands that I immerse myself in that natural thermal water at least every two weeks. In Spain, I relish the Turkish-type hamman slabs of hot marble. I also connect with the local community to find someone who does physical body work, be it an osteopath, a chiropractor, a body-talk practitioner or good old-fashioned massage. I ensure that every two weeks I engage in some body work. I know that might seem like a lot, but when your life and livelihood depend on you being in peak health and on top of your game, you have to make it a priority. At least, I do.

Mind and heart

Sometimes living #LocationFree might mean spending a lot more time on your own, or having to navigate new transport systems in foreign countries, or figuring out access to properties at night, finding yourself in a brand-new community where you know no one. When you are in different time zones you might not always be able to easily call someone you know up for help. So you absolutely need to be mentally alert and vigilant and have the right support systems in place.

I am not sure about you, but I also have a history of allowing internal stress to develop into depression. I understand the "black dog" pretty well, and know the cycles in which it works and the havoc it can wreak in its wake. To this day, I find I have had to be extra careful about who I hang out with, the friendships I nurture, how I handle my intimate relationship, the money aspect of life, and generally be quite strict about keeping myself mentally and emotionally healthy.

Instead of a doctor, I have a homeopath. My longstanding, trusted homeopath friend moved to the USA with his family. Then, at one point in my first year, I knew was in some trouble health wise because I was really battling with menopause, asthma and depression. So I got him on a Skype call and he was able to tell me what to get when I was in the UK. So here was my South African homeopath speaking from the USA telling me what to do in the UK. He helped get me emotionally strong again – there is always a way.

Over the last few years, I had a second homeopath in Johannesburg and every time I was there I'd make sure I see him. I also started being a little more pre-emptive and would get three months' worth of supplements and remedies to take with me. Ultimate self-care meant being proactive, prepared and willing. For me, it has meant owning up to my vulnerabilities, my weaknesses, and being willing to ask for support when I felt I needed it.

When you live in a neighbourhood you're familiar with, there is a certain level of comfort in "knowing" that you can reach out to your circle, visit a friend, pop to the pharmacy, nip in to see your doctor. That's very different when living #LocationFree, and is something to figure out early on in your journey. This is even more important if you are on heavier prescription drugs, or hormone replacement treatment. Don't assume you can get everything you need in different countries. Do your homework and be very strict about this.

Annual appointments are great if you happen to return to a base that you know better than any other. Use that time to get all your regular check-ups: doctor, dentist, gynae, mammogram and prostate check, for example. In this way, you tune up as you go. I did that that every time I was in South Africa.

Another part of mental health is taking down time. It can be too easy for me to get stuck into full-time work mode, sitting behind my Mac holding client sessions online, writing, getting admin done or handling marketing. So, when arriving in a new place, I set myself little targets of how much time to take off each week. I block out down time and play time in my diary. It might be to visit a specific museum, sit on a plaza sipping coffee or wine, or simply watching the world unfold before me. I have learned the art of slowing down and simply being. Of not having to rush everywhere all the time.

I laugh at myself when I think of the dichotomy that is my business brand ("The Quick Shift Deva") and the fact that I am learning the absolute necessity of slowing down! This means being more deliberate, intentional and doing less. More real time off, saying no and not having to always fill my schedule with every minute taken care of. What would be the point of being in wonderfully exciting and new communities to explore if all I am going to do is work? Round the world in 80 days is *not* what I am aiming for.

Emotional and mental health is also deeply impacted by the condition of your body. I found that the more I had the body stuff under control, the easier it was for me to stay on an even keel. I am by nature quite emotional and experience the peaks of highs and the depths of lows. As mentioned in my ritual steps (*see* Lesson 5), one of my go-to tools is journaling. Actively writing by hand has served me well since I was 13 years old, a way for me to process what is going on around me. Sometimes it's a mind dump, a purge that gets all the crap out; sometimes intentional goal setting, or some spiritual conscious work. There are also other coaching tools I use to heal, such as the Emotional Freedom Technique (EFT) or Neuro-Linguistic Programming (NLP). EFT is my go-to miracle worker when I need to process and shift emotions rather than stuff them away or pretend they're not there. *Out* is always better than *in*!

One of the most underrated ways of healing mind and heart is simply reaching out and asking for support. Once, when I was in San Francisco for a three-month exploration stint, I was feeling seriously out of whack. It was a particularly trying time. I was lonely (even though I was still in my committed relationship), depressed, out of kilter and felt close to suicidal. I have never been at the stage where I would actually do anything to harm myself, but I was feeling so f***ing bad about everything that for the briefest moment I entertained suicidal thoughts. I knew, of course, that I could never actually go through with it, and nor did I ever want to; rather, it was a question of not wanting to be here.

I immediately reached out to someone I knew who did energy healing, and went about setting myself up an appointment. But, despite everything I did to try to make this appointment, I was blocked at every turn. Now, there are times when you need to take that as a sign that you should not go ahead, but I knew with absolute certainty that I needed to have a session with this healer. I was hellbent on it – it was a lifeline for me.

He was in Cape Town and I was in San Francisco. Everything seemed to be conspiring against us, but literally five minutes before the designated time we finally made contact and it all fell into place. I cried with relief when he tapped into my energy body and was able to help me figure out what was going on emotionally, mentally and spiritually. I cried for another 24 hours as I processed it all, and only then did I start to feel better. To this day, I have never fallen as far down that awful dark hole as I did that day. I also know that if I even start heading that way and slipping down that slope, I book another appointment and get my tune up. There is no shame in needing help!

I have a handful of people I reach out to – a homeopath, spiritual healer, body talk practitioner, chiropractor who reads energy fields, Vedic-based astrologer. There are friends and family too, of course, as well as other forms of support I find in the communities I infiltrate.

No, dear reader, I am not some wacko living in La-la Land – I have my feet firmly on the ground and know what modality to use and when to use it. I believe in giving myself the best opportunity of staying strong, balanced, level headed and engaged, so that I can contribute more to the world and be able to both give and receive in every way conceivable.

Spirit

My regular practice of yoga is also a spiritual practice for me. Far from being religious in nature, yoga simply means the *yoke*, or union, of body and mind. Every time I practise yoga I am checking in with and connecting to my spiritual side. It allows me to take a very deep and expansive breath – even when the position, or asanas, are extremely challenging. The busier I was for work, the more I would opt for the more restorative yin-type practices. The quieter I was at work, the more I would opt for the rigorous and challenging styles of Bikram, flow and hatha. Again, it's about knowing which form for when. Which style is ideal for your energy at the time? No right or wrong, simply what is appropriate in that moment for your needs.

I also love to use the flying time as a form of spiritual connection for me, an opportunity to check in with myself, tap in to who I am and what on earth I am doing with my life. I like to play little games: I use the time on a long-haul flight to visualise myself flying high above my life and looking down on it, able to see things with different perspective and insight. I use that opportunity for more strategic thinking time, rather than the smaller, day-to-day stuff. I may, for instance, plan the next year, or contemplate a business idea, or brainstorm a book. I also have a little ritual every time the plane takes off or lands. I uncross my arms and legs as the plane hurtles down the runway and lifts into the air and give thanks and send a prayer of gratitude into the world. I repeat that up until the seatbelt sign goes off. I do the same when we come in to land. I have never had anxiety about travelling or flying, so I don't do it to quell that; it's simply a ritual I have built into my life that is all about mindfulness and intention.

If on a bus or train, I might use that time for something a little closer to the ground, perhaps figuring out what is stopping me from feeling grounded, or tripping me up. I have always loved staring out a window at a moving landscape; it is a deeply contemplative time for me – or what you might call meditation. Allow the rhythm of the train or bus to become a type of mantra or white noise.

I have four of my own personal mantras that I rinse and repeat. These are deep personal prayers that are locked in. The first came to me about 18 years ago after I had travelled solo in my little convertible VW Beetle cross country in South Africa with about ZAR100 to my name. Nearing my destination, I stopped 10 kilometres short of the village, just when I spotted the first sign to the turn-off to Barrydale, and it literally came to me. That personal mantra is: "Oh infinite Spirit, I am willing to experience the truth of my Divine Plan." Repeating it is like a soothing ice-cream lolly on a hot day.

Another mantra was given to me in Sanskrit and English when I was rambling across the Klein Karoo on a 10-day walkabout. A fourth one when I was trying to run up a steep hill when I was not very fit, and the repetition of it somehow kept me going up-up-*up* that hill to the light at the top of a lemon grove. That one is as follows:

If I choose to then I want to,

If I want to then I can,

If I can I must, and
If I must I will!

There is power in those words for me!

Meditation is another of my support measures. I cannot pretend I am any kind of meditation guru or even follow any particular meditation practice. I just do my best. I have done several meditation and contemplation classes; every year, for example, I participate in the Deepak Chopra/Oprah collaborations. I also love the Abraham Hicks teachings. We each have to find what works for us and seek out that community of support as we travel! When I resonate particularly with something, I will be sure to purchase it to re-use often.

Sometimes I just sit quietly, with my eyes closed, doing my best to focus on the breath and stay calm. I choose one of the breathing techniques I have learned over the years, but I have found that the process is an organic one for me – it's more about remembering to do it and embracing the benefits in the moments than having one specific thing I do.

I would love to hear about *your* personal rituals. Do you have favourite mantras, prayers or affirmations that keep you connected?

 **WHAT OTHERS SAY ABOUT ...**

The LAY Principle

I have my daily and weekly rituals, which involve yoga, journaling and meditation. I'm fortunate to live near the beach here in Malaga and so get lots of long walks in, which are an essential part of looking after my mental and physical wellbeing. Use a comparison website like Expatica.com to help you to find quotes for insurance. I feel like it's easier now than ever to be able to eat well when you're travelling and to find places that cater to different dietary requirements. The same goes for exercise. I'm a big yoga fan and it doesn't matter where I am in the world, there will always be a yoga class I can go to.

I tend to use specific herb-based sleeping products like pillow spray with lavender to help me to relax and sleep well.

—Victoria Jane Watson

Routine is the best framework to apply in the beginning. You might need to tweak it as you settle into a new environment, but it ultimately helps you get you settled. I needed to wait 90 days before I qualified for medical insurance. You do need to look at this as a crucial factor. While it is wonderful to be travelling and living light and out of a suitcase, if something goes wrong, that can truly take the best-planned opportunity and turn it right on its head. I believe you need a hospital plan, as the sniffles and small items can often be dealt with locally where ever you are, but should a bigger medical issue arrive, you don't want to be out of funds and insurance in a foreign country.

I am a person who walks, so my routine has included counting steps or walking to places of interest. I include my exercise as part of the journey, as you often explore new places more authentically when you are walking among the locals. I am quite adventurous with food, and like to try new things. In fact, many a memory is due to a new experience.

Allow for the jet lag if you are flying across time zones. Be mindful that you might very well need a full day of orientation or rest for your body to start finding its new cadence.

—Deborah Louise Botha

Time zones don't particularly bother me, I listen to my body about sleep; if I need to sleep, I will ... I remember working in Indonesia and after lunch the participants of the workshop were all dozing off - I asked my interpreter if I was doing something wrong and he said, "The body does what the body needs," and that was that ... I try to follow that mantra! I do notice that going "with" the spin of the world (Australia to UK), I can land and go straight to work; when I'm going "against" time, the jetlag is harder and longer, so I need to make sure I accommodate for that in my diary bookings!

Different beds are weekly and also why I tend to prefer hotels because they have standards - I have slept at friends' houses where I had to get up in the middle of the night to find "anything" to pad/stuff the bedding for more comfort; there are also places I return to where I know what to do, i.e. an Indian complex where I know that the sofa lounge folds out like a bed is more comfy to put on top of the hard Indian bed to sleep on.

—Dee Brooks

In terms of staying in my best mental and physical state, I read a lot. I read at least a book every three days. Usually, the books are about mental, physical or financial illness. I'll usually throw in a biography as well once in a while, but I read at least an hour or two every day and that really just keeps me tuned up. In terms of eating and exercise, I work out six times a week. During this quarantine time period, I was been doing a lot of home workouts, but typically I'll go to a gym. Whenever I move to a new place, the first things I look for before getting there are the gyms and the co-working spaces because that's what I need to feel settled (less so an apartment). If I know a co-working space that I'm going to like and I know a gym that I'll like, then I feel settled.

I don't sleep very much. I sleep probably five hours a night on average, maybe six, but I've just never needed much sleep. But, yeah, in terms of taking time out, I definitely maintain having that connection with myself so that if I am not feeling at 100% efficiency, then I take some time off.

—**Gene Ellis**

My work is abundance: physical, emotional, mental and, the most important, spiritual health. Meditations, Tai Chi and yoga. Teeth should be checked regularly. I don't take any medication and I work with the world's leading company for cellular nutrition (highest European/German quality organic), available worldwide, thus no problems to get it anywhere I am and no need to carry huge amounts with me.

I eat preferably organic, local and from the season. If organic is not possible, I always prefer fresh and seasonal than processed and in plastic.

Exercise is important. I suffer 24-hour pain from an accident, thus my body needs to be stretched and oxygenated.

I always sleep well as long as it is not too noisy, though I normally chose places that are suitable for me. My cellular nutrition helps for a deep, profound rest.

Beds can be a challenge, because I am tall and I don't like them very soft ... lol. Normally, I am lucky, and if not, then just ask or find something better – there is always a solution. Different time zones might be a bit tiring over the first days when changing, but then it's fine. Also exercises from my Daoist work help to adapt very quickly.

—**Nabila Welk**

Our medical insurance was with IMG Europe (their Global Fusion policy) and I kept the premiums low by opting for a large excess, but I obtained quotes from other providers. Whilst the UK was in the EU, we could access member countries' state emergency medical treatment via the EHIC (European Health Insurance Card). Therefore, the private insurance would be for serious health problems, or repatriation and I always ensured we had savings to cover the excess funds.

We have used the EHIC and also, for ease, on occasion we've paid at private clinics too. Farmacias are the initial port of call though, as some treatments that can only be bought on prescription in the UK are available over the counter in Spain – until recently, Rob's asthma inhalers, for example. Herboristeria stores are also very helpful for alternative treatments and supplements.

Following an unexpected pulmonary embolism in spring 2019, I take anticoagulants and a month's pack on prescription is just 19 cents. The hospital treatment and follow-up healthcare I received was excellent, with the biggest challenge being the language barrier. Needing to access ongoing doctors' and hospital appointments is the main reason we stayed in Spain for the last 12 months, but we plan to be back on our travels sometime in the future.

—Nancy Benn

A few years ago I learned the practice of transcendental meditation (TM).

This helps the mind, body, and soul in any circumstance. I also always have an A5 booklet/journal and pen with me, and writing about a situation, thoughts, feelings, and ideas is a great way for me to feel grounded. I don't take any medications and, in the case of injury, I'm covered by my insurance. I always travel with a bottle of tea-tree oil, a bottle of Echinaforce, and a jar of coconut oil. In all of my years, that's been enough. I eat a mainly vegetarian diet and am very selective about the places where I'll eat fish and sometimes chicken. Lots of walking, water, light yoga and breathing exercises every other day also help.

I travel with a bag of oats in my vanity so that I can always have something nutritious and filling by simply adding water. I mostly eat fresh, natural and local wherever I am. I don't try to find the same foods I eat at home. I keep it simple and stock up on fruits and vegetables and try to eat out only once a day.

I can sleep pretty much anywhere (TM helps for that too). When entering a new time zone, I wake for the first sunrise and, facing the sun, sit quietly or meditate. Sometimes I go back to bed for a few hours, but that first sunrise seems to get you adjusted pretty quickly.

—**Lynne Scullard**

I have to do a cardio workout everyday. This can be challenging when I don't have access to a gym, so I will use online videos. Take what medication or supplements you need with you. Eating can also be challenging, particularly since I'm vegetarian, but I feel like a lot of places that used to be pretty veg unfriendly have really evolved, like Medellin and Buenos Aires. I try to cook a reasonable amount. Beds can be challenging and I've taken a mattress topper with me once and I'm glad I did.

—**Uday Jhunjhunwala**

Finally, the question that allows me to give my personal Top Tip!

I meditate … Sitting down on a cushion, or if it suits you better, during a hike, the dishwashing or having a bath. If you can't meditate (or think you can't), make time to do nothing and just be bored. Both activities (though one a bit more skilful then the other) will allow you to get in touch with what is happening within yourself, instead of reacting to the outside world.

To be honest, I am not very good at maintaining a daily sitting meditation practice myself, but I do meditate often in times of waiting for a train or something, or it happens on its own when I am doing something repetitive like hiking or dishwashing.

And as one of my more (in)famous teachers once said: "If your whole life falls apart, the only thing you have to put back together is your meditation practice, and everything else will follow." This advice I remembered when my life was falling apart (or so I thought), and following it made a huge difference in my life …

I am a firm believer of living healthy instead of medicating. So listen to your body when you eat, and adjust your diet accordingly. This for me means little to no wheat/gluten or regular milk or certain kinds of meat, and I try to be sensible with my sugar intake. Without it, I have more energy, have over time lost 13 kilograms, and generally am and feel much happier.

Oh, and it helps if you find enjoyment in cooking! This way, you can eat something put together from actual foods like potatoes, vegetables fish/meat etcetera, instead of eating prepackaged "food" with all sorts of chemical preservatives, additives, sugar/fat/ replacements etcetera. Like an American food professor once said: "If you need to be a scientist to understand what you are eating, you probably shouldn't eat it."

—**Martin van den Berg**

I am my best friend and regularly ask myself, "Is my life as good as it can be? If not, then what can I do for me right now that would make it better?" I eat plant-based 90% of the time, so I am almost never sick. An anti-inflammatory diet means my body is strong and has a strong immune system. I use coconut oil instead of toothpaste as it is antibacterial and takes away any small infections or holes that might show up. I never eat refined sugar or food with refined sugar if I can avoid it. I use a flavourless honey in my coffee if I can get it. If I need a snack, I'll eat nuts and berries.

Beds are a thing. The older I get the harder it is for me to just accept what may be considered a good bed. So I never book more than one to two nights in a place and then spend time walking around talking to hosts and looking at the beds, so I can find one that suits me.

—**Mette Glargaard**

I'm a yoga practitioner. Fortunately, I have been doing that for many years of my life and I can comfortably do a home practice without needing instruction. So that's my go-to. I'm really addicted at the moment to walking. I have an app on my phone that's measuring my steps and I'm excited about that. And that is, generally speaking, my go-to mode in any city: my feet. And I will happily walk for four or five hours to get to where I want to go. So I purposefully avoid metros and buses and things so that I can exercise and walk because my body enjoys that.

And then the eating aspect, I guess, that part of my self-care is bringing myself down to a very simple diet that keeps me from getting stomach bugs and nonsense that I don't want to have to deal with. I'm generally a very healthy person. I have a great medical insurance that I rely on if I feel like I'm going to get into trouble.

Now that I have this permanent visa in Chile, I'm plugged into the medical system so I have annual dental care and I've had medical check-ups, but I also believe in self-healing. So if I sense in any spot of my body that something's not cool, I'll focus in and concentrate on that and try and do some self-healing for a couple of days and I've been quite successful with that. The biggest thing I feel that impacts my health when I travel is changing weather conditions because you're moving in different altitudes.

And that's also where the packing and the wardrobe comes in because you've got to make sure that you're ready if you find yourself five hours into a bus ride and all of a sudden the temperature's changed and you're freezing your butt off. You've got to have the perfect gear for that. And you've got to take care of yourself because it's those conditions that can impact your health.

—Michelle Clarke

The feeling of having control over your work hours, income level and plans of life and the future in general is important, I think. If you have to worry constantly over money, it affects your peace of mind significantly. To have maximum time to myself, I have chosen a well-paying job and the income level of Northern Europe, but I spend my money in Southern Europe, which means that my expenses are about 50% less compared to my home country. This means I can afford to work only half a day and have the rest of the day to my family and myself. I only work three to four hours per day. I'm also in full control of my working hours. During my work week, I do outdoor activities, exercise, spend time with family, meet with friends, go out to parties and cultural activities. I never work on weekends and I take little holidays often. The only downside of my job is that the tax office expects monthly reporting, so it's hard for me to take more than two or three weeks of holiday uninterrupted.

—Katia Enbuske

I'm insured in the Netherlands with an obligated healthcare insurance and voluntary travellers' insurance. I'm a lucky man that I don't need regular medication. Once I used some medication against a skin disease, but I stopped this medication before I started my travel. It's not life threatening, so I can live without. Sunshine, stress-less life and sea will help avoiding it.

In the Netherlands I never did sports, so while travelling I don't either. During my travel I learned something very important: looking at food in a different way. I don't eat sugar, pasta, white bread and fried things any more and over the months I lost 8 kilograms of weight with this!

—**Jan van Kuijk**

 # WHAT OTHERS SAY ABOUT ...

Taking time out

I always allow myself a full day a week to explore and attempt different things that are on offer in whichever country we dock. There is nothing nicer than exploring and finding a quaint little coffee shop that serves something you truly enjoy, and being able to revisit it and weave it into your story.

—**Deborah Louise Botha**

Your body will tell you when you need some time out. I just take it without apology. For me, it's a long walk, some time in nature/a park/a place with a view, or simply a quiet meal on my own in a beautiful restaurant, preferably with a view. I'm completely in love with sunsets.

—**Lynne Scullard**

One of the first things we do when we get to a new place is find out where the local market is. Markets are the best places to get produce, always great fresh fruits and veggies at great prices. Also, the money you pay them goes to the farmers, not corporations.

Usually we go for walks and do yoga, but it can take a bit of work to get the routine going. Walks and hikes are no problem to do; the actual work is getting the yoga routine going. Not all places we stay have yoga studios nearby, or sometimes they don't have a very good space for it. But it's possible with focus and dedication.

We don't have travel insurance, but we stay in shape and eat really well and rarely need to see a doctor because of this. In some countries you don't need to see a doctor to get antibiotics, or other medications. This can be good and bad, depending on the situation.

Sometimes you just need something to fix your stomach; those pharmacists have a pretty good medical training and so they can just give you what you need without a prescription. However, this can lead to irresponsible self-diagnosis, and you might not actually be fixing what is really wrong with you. Another bonus is that the prices of meds are usually pretty good in these countries.

The quality of beds varies greatly, but we've been lucky to have mostly slept on amazingly comfortable beds. There is the odd time that we have to sleep on what's comparable to a plank, but these character-building moments help you appreciate the beauty of comfort even more.

Getting sufficient rest is important to your health as well. We make our own schedules, so usually we wake up on our own. Sometimes it's 10 am, sometimes it's noon. We found that we're happier if we wake up naturally, as opposed to being woken up by an alarm.

I've noticed two things that created needless stress in our lives in Canada. One is waking up with an alarm, the other is being cold. When you live in areas where you don't have to worry about being cold and needing to stay warm, it's so much easier on your mind. It's just another layer of stress you don't need to have.

—Chris de Cap

I used a mobile fitness app called Freeletics to keep in shape. It's great because it requires space outdoors, which makes you scan your neighbourhood to look for a suitable flat surface. I have exercised in football stadiums, on a baseball pitch, on a basketball court, and on beaches.

Any high-intensive interval training will do for this. I loved starting my work day after an intensive workout.

—André Gussekloo

Carve out time in your schedule for relaxation and do it at a time that works for you. For example, I like to take a walk in the afternoon if I can to break up the day and reset my energy.

—Victoria Jane Watson

With the risk of repeating myself, do what makes you happy, not what should make you happy or what someone else tells you will make you happy. Be open to what comes on your path, and embrace that which fits you better than what is currently in your life.

—Martin van den Berg

I normally stay in hostels or homestays and then, once a month or so, I will stay at a nice hotel for a night or two and be pampered. If I can get a massage I will most certainly do that.

—Mette Glargaard

Hmm ... You know, I was in a relationship and in that period I could take time for us and I enjoyed that. Now that I'm single it's just less important to me.

—Jan van Kuijk

My sense of taking care of myself has increased tenfold in this lifestyle. I take a great responsibility in taking care of myself because I need to come back to work. So if I'm going to go out and explore a city, but I have a four o'clock appointment with a client, I can't take undue risks because I must be back to serve my client. So, I avoid dangerous areas. If ever I feel I'm in danger, I'll take immediate action. I'm very alert, very aware and very protective of my stuff.

I'm also open, I meet strangers, I'm spontaneous, but my degree of Michelle – be responsible for Michelle – is very heightened and I'm pleased about that.

—Michelle Clarke

I started this journey broken ... I've had almost five years of crawling out of the hole of depression and post-traumatic stress disorder and it's been tough, but I could not have done it at the family home – it's been slow and steady, sometimes five steps forward and 10 steps back ... My daily practices have waxed and waned in response to my emotional motivation and yet, I'm currently feeling more together and well than I have in a decade!

My main tip would be to try to be kind to yourself – always! When the negative voices entered my head to tell me how shit I was, I would reply with kindness and almost speak to that other voice as someone else and tell them to stop, be kind, loving and present ... It didn't always work, but each day, bit by bit, it's got me to a good place now!

We are lucky in Australia to have Medicare so I don't need private medical insurance and my travel insurance covers the rest. I don't have any regular medications I need, although there is a natural supplement I take for my scoliosis and that has been tricky to find at times – I have developed a habit of buying too much when I see it and I haven't run out again lately. I also sometimes change my travel route to ensure I go via either of the chiropractors where I can get adjusted and buy some of the natural tablets.

Eating well and exercise is abundantly available; it's my mental health or body pains that stops me at times. I have walking apps, eating apps, meditation apps, writing apps, and I just have to convince myself daily to use them, which is easier on quiet days and harder (or easier to ignore) on busy days.

Taking time out is so important! I'm currently on a four-week break to recharge the batteries for the coming year and I'm staying with a friend in a self-contained cottage on her property. During work times, I try to never book back-to-back work and always have a day or two each side of each piece of work to explore the place that I'm in and soak it up!

—Dee Brooks

I have a rule that "I'm the prize" and my self-care (mental and physical wellbeing) is the most important thing. I actively build this into my life first.

Sleep is my main priority and I'm gentle on myself if I don't get enough. I always have earplugs with me and meditate before bed with them in. I live in the centre of a very busy city so they're really important!

I get outside once a day at least. I try to have a conversation with someone every day, as I love talking! Water ... at least two to three litres a day. I take multivitamins, drink sleepy-time mushroom tea, eat well and still love a bit of cake. My workout is either walking or resistance bands. Those are awesome for travelling. I also pack my intuition deck cards for when I need some guidance. I meditate most days and I journal religiously.

I'm a mission-driven human so my work is important to me, but I always put myself first.

—Carolynne Alexander

Rob worked part-time in England on a zero-hours contract, which was why it was easy for him to stop work and travel, so we were used to spending time at home together. He's my soul mate and we rub along nicely day to day. I work and he cooks and drives the long distances, whilst we tend to go food shopping together because translating the products is always an interesting challenge.

As I worked from home for many years before travelling, I'm also used to working remotely and alone. If I have a wobble, I talk to someone. My kids are adults and we have a good relationship; I have friends in the UK and also in Spain, and I'm in regular contact with clients and have other VA colleagues for support. So far, I've not felt the need to climb aboard a plane to go "home" at times other than the scheduled visits.

My main exercise comes from taking the dogs for a walk, but I do a little yoga at home and swim whenever we're in a house with a pool (luxury), or live near the sea or a lake. Sleep can vary due to different beds in our various homes but, generally, we've found the quality of mattresses to be good. It's usually the heat or mosquitoes that keep us awake!

Rob and I have always enjoyed a varied diet (and he's an experimental cook) so don't really miss the English staples and prepare meals with what's available locally. There's a wonderful selection of fresh fruit and vegetables here, which are cheaper on the market than can be bought in the UK. This suits us as we're vegetarians and it's easier to prepare our own meals than eat out because Spanish and Portuguese menus tend to be very meat oriented.

In the two-plus years we've been travelling, we've taken one holiday, visiting friends in Ireland. We could find pet sitters in plenty of time as we had an annual rental due to my needing to remain in Valencia for a year for medical reasons. After a hot dry summer, we opted for a two-week holiday in a damp green Ireland in September! The rest of the time, we live in such beautiful surroundings that I deliberately don't work Friday afternoons and start my weekend early. We go exploring to historical towns, walking and swimming, so feel each weekend is a relaxing mini holiday. I have a flexible work pattern as I decide when to work, so I build relaxation time into my diary on a regular basis. All European countries have more public holidays than the UK so there's usually a celebration or fiesta to enjoy most weeks!

—**Nancy Benn**

 **TOP TIPS!**

- Nurturing yourself needs to be your priority.
- Learn to love your own company.
- Asking for help and support takes courage, but pays off.

Navigating relationships and building community

ONE OF THE QUESTIONS I am asked over and over again is: "But, Kate, don't you get lonely?" "Well, yes, for sure I do, sometimes even debilitatingly so, but doesn't everyone?" Don't you also get lonely living in your own house and neighbourhood and going about your regular life? Times when you wonder where everyone is, or why a friend hasn't been in touch?

Life is the interplay between solo time and being connected to others. We are always shifting between the two. Some of us prefer more time with other people (which, as you already know, does not necessarily negate the sense of loneliness), while others prefer more alone time. It's the dance between the two that has always fascinated me, and so I start this chapter by talking about the more intimate relationships in our lives: with a partner, family and friends.

Intimate partner

When I started on this journey, I was in a relatively new relationship. I had told him the first night we met that I travelled a lot and would be leaving to live in another county at some point in the near future. We had only been dating for seven months when the time came, but his answer to me was always the same: You go and I will follow. I trusted that. We had to start synching our diaries a little more to accommodate the greater rhythm – sometimes we hit the jackpot and sometimes we didn't.

He was completely supportive of my #LocationFree choice; in fact, it seemed to suit him to have a little space and time apart. Some years we were great at planning ahead and making time and would meet somewhere for special holidays, exploring and playing. About three or four times a year I would go to South Africa. He was still very active in his businesses, so perhaps my being away gave him the freedom and time to focus. Looking back, I honestly loved the anchor of being in a relationship with him. It felt solid, stabilising, nurturing and supportive. We didn't have a set routine as to how we would connect when we were apart, but mostly it was WhatsApp and Skype chats. I was definitely the one who wanted and needed more connection – ironic when I am the one who chose this itinerant lifestyle, huh?

By the time I completed this book in Scotland, five years down the line, I was single. We separated just under a year previously. The gods had other plans for us. We all need anchors and witnesses in life, and during our time together he provided that for me. I hold our love dear in my heart and always will, regardless of the outcome. If you have read any of my other books or blogs, he appears many times – my Argentinian 007 with whom I danced through life. One of my most treasured memories was that, unless he absolutely couldn't, I knew he would be the one waiting for me as I walked out through International Arrivals at Johannesburg, ready to embrace me, no matter what time of day or night.

Looking back with wisdom, compassion and love, I see so many ways in which we could have done it differently. But then I always return to the notion of trust: trust in the process and the decisions we have both made, whether those be active or passive – by which I mean that sometimes not making a decision or taking action is in itself a decision. The greater irony is that I started writing this book shortly after we separated, at a time when I was deeply sad, feeling as though as I had failed. That somehow I had messed up and that my lifestyle came first over our relationship. In truth, our relationship was always more important than the lifestyle, but we were unable to find a way through all of that.

As with so much of life, I know it is simply about one day at a time. I do not know what the future holds for me in terms of a life partner yet – perhaps I will make my next book a sizzling romance set in Italy.

Friends

One of the greatest comforts in my life has been Stripey, my cat, and it was really hard for me to say goodbye when he went to his new forever home with a dear friend. The moment I knew he had settled in, however, my heart rested easier. Many will criticise the decision to leave Stripey, but I came to terms with that kind of loss many, many years ago. I had my first cat at age 10, a beautiful lilac-pointed Siamese named Azure Dee. He was killed just two years later … Can you imagine, at 12 years old, being told that your beloved fur baby was found slaughtered and left on the doorstep when I was away at boarding school. I was heartbroken and sobbed my entire Easter holiday! Since then, I have had a gazillion animals in and out of my life. When friends' parents got divorced, or abandoned animals needed a home, or a beautiful Staffie needed loving because his owners were about to lose everything they had, I have simply said yes to giving them a home. I always try to let my heart and intuition guide me, knowing that four-legged beauties come in and out of our lives. I love deeply – oh so, deeply – but I also know it's okay to let them move to another home. When I have become their new caregiver, I have seen first hand how fast animals adapt, so I allow myself to be soothed by that when I have had to do the same.

I still carry heartache around it, of course, but we all have to find ways to make peace with our decisions as best we can. Once I knew that Stripey would have three humans and another kitty to love and to love him back, rather than watch me leave and then stay away for six months at a time, I felt infinitely more at peace and was then able to share my new lifestyle with my friends.

Having being privy to so many of my off-the-wall ideas in the past, they were instantly excited. The most common response was, "Yippee! We're so happy for you – how exciting! But when are you coming back, Kate? When will we share a glass of wine and a laugh?" Of course, most just assumed that I was simply going on a long holiday as opposed to a lifestyle choice unfolding.

Family

At the time of shifting gears, all my immediate family was in the UK, so my decision didn't really matter to them one way or another. I am super close to my mum, and every year we find a way to make sure we hang out and connect – she would visit me to celebrate a birthday, for instance, and we would meet annually in Greece or I would visit her at her home. Spending special occasions with the whole family together is not a big thing in our family, but making sure I carved out the time to see my mum was vital.

I found a way to try to work around big celebrations, and because my partner was also family now, we factored in that too. I was always with him for our respective birthdays and Valentine's Day and, when the time came, I made sure that I was able to spend my mum's eightieth birthday with her. In the same breath, I have also spent some Christmas and New Year entirely on my own, or I would find a version of "family" wherever I was to celebrate with. Remember the story in Lesson 3 of my Christmas spent volunteering in Malaga? We all have to find the rhythm of our year that works for us, one that feeds our hearts and souls. There is no one right or wrong way – just the way that calls to you.

Community and connection

Social media is another interesting factor we have to consider now. We look in on others people's lives and make an instant assumption about them and their lives or how they are doing on the success scale. One of my most steadfast values is honesty, so I have always done my level best to be super open, honest and vulnerable – like sharing here about my depression. I am all about authenticity and not buying the social media mask that makes everyone feel less than, worthless and uncool. Or sets us up for negative comparisons.

Since living my #LocationFree life, I have gone through phases with social media. There are times when I post a lot and feel way more engaged, but then there are times when I am silent, introspective and just do my own thing away from the glare of social media, when I simply don't feel I need to share with anyone.

I have always had a newsletter and have blogged throughout the last 17 years since starting my professional life-coaching business. At the beginning of the #LocationFree lifestyle choice, I came up with the hashtag #TheMinimalistManifesto. I assumed I would be blogging a lot more about my journey. I even contemplated starting a proper travel blog and using it as a way to earn income, but in truth I have probably written less in this last phase of life #LocationFree – I have been busy living it, being in it.

At the end of my first year, after some training with the YPO, I was in the UK for three months with my mum, and spent some time looking after a beautiful kitty in the centre of London. I walked for hours every day in the cold, rain, and winter and loved it. My mum had lent me her white Russian fluffy hat, and I felt quite exotic in the greyness of the streets of London. But I was also miserable about my business and coaching in general, wondering whether I still had the energy, passion or drive to run my business with success.

Everything felt bland and boring, and yet I was feeling healthy and relatively strong, not depressed, no self-pity. I sat with this for a while ... What on earth was going on? So I played the game I play with clients by asking the question: "How long do you feel you could still commit to this?" You start by asking yourself whether you could commit to a point far into the future; for me, that was five years. And I *knew* at that point that I could not commit to my coaching business for another five years. "And what about just three years?" No. I was tired, disinterested, bored and a little burnt out – but emotionally strong, I thought. Even though there were some awesome developments unfolding for me, I was simply falling out of love with my business.

So it came down to the fact that I could commit to my business until my fiftieth birthday, which was just 16 months away. That felt like a milestone I could reach, and I gave myself permission to recommit, re-energise and get wholeheartedly stuck back in, knowing I had a cut-off point. I then gave myself permission to do a significant re-evaluation around my fiftieth birthday.

Once I had given myself a much shorter time frame that was believable and felt doable, I was able to relax into it again. It was at that point that I found two fun new apps on my iPhone to do some cool stuff to photos. I started a series of posts where I take a photo and digitally·alter it to make it funkier and place inspirational text on top. That gave me the boost I needed to be able to share something of myself again in the world of social media. I still take regular breaks from social media, but that is juxtaposed with knowing that it is a vital part of my business. In 2020 I spent a lot of time offline not connecting with my larger community, doing inner retreat work for myself instead.

Using Facebook for groups has been integral to staying connected to my clients, family and friends. I run a private Facebook group for my coaching community, and have several groups for our writing mentorships and retreats. At one point, I also used Slack as a platform for Masterminds, but found it less user friendly, and reverted back to Facebook – for now anyway.

I found that it has been fairly easy to manage my clients from the #LocationFree space. I have always ensured that my business was able to function in a more online way, with occasional face-to-face sessions, and that has been especially important when it came to one of the most important shifts in the last five years: how long I would stay for each trip to South Africa.

I had to start weaning friends and clients off them depending on me and when I would be there to interact with them face to face. That was tough for me to manage. I started saying yes to less and less face-to-face work, so the obligation to be there lessened. I had grown to love the northern hemisphere more and more and felt my energy being pulled there.

Where does your energy naturally pull you? If you were to introduce living #LocationFree to your community of friends and clients, what do you feel would be their greatest resistance or your biggest block? The truth is you will have to navigate those complicated emotions for yourself in order to give yourself permission to live that way.

Technology to stay connected

Nowadays, using technology means you never have to feel too far from anyone. I make a point of staying tuned in to friends with regular WhatsApp messages, staying up to date on their social media profiles to keep up with them, and making time to chat regularly. Nurturing people is very important to my mental health. If I was just popping in for a casual "hello", I would usually just make a WhatsApp call or drop a quick voice note; WhatsApp is such an easy platform for that. One of my clients introduced me to another app Marco Polo, which allows you to leave live video messages for each other – perhaps even more personal than a voice note.

I also ensure that I carve out times to do a longer check-in with each other. We might then have an hour chat while sipping some wine together in different countries, really delving deeper into each other's lives. Often one of us might need more airtime and TLC than the other. I love the ebb and flow of how we let the other talk and how we stay connected. These are usually on Skype or Zoom. My mum and I also do voice notes and WhatsApp calls, or Skype (yes, at 81, she is a truly modern octogenarian).

I really do make time to tune in and stay connected to my community of support, both for my own peace of mind and to assure them that I am here for them. It also helps me to feel held and that I can reach out no matter the geography!

I have just one simple rule: Anytime that anyone pops into my space, I will reach out and say hi. Often when travelling I will see something that reminds me of a particular person, and I will take a pic and pop them a message. For the long-distance friends I have met over the years through travel and work, every few months I might prod them – or be prodded – and say, "Hey, long time … Let's chat." And then we book a proper appointment to chat and connect. I find that having it in my diary is a really big help. My singular aim is to feel connected and connecting, supported and supporting, loved and loving, heard and listening. I do what needs to be done to hold that together in any way I can.

I find, too, that I need to be more vigilant when in different time zones. When I know someone is having a really tough time, I keep dropping him or her little voice notes of support so that they get them when they wake up. Those are what got me through some of my toughest weeks, darkest times and WTF moments – waking up to a message of love from someone thinking about me across the miles. That web of energy connecting us all. How do you stay connected and plugged in so that you don't feel isolated and alone?

By the same token, if I am going to go into retreat or silent mode, I make sure I let certain people know, and assure them that I will check my phone once a day in case of emergency if I am somewhere remote or isolated. That way, they feel safe knowing that I am safe and they know that if an emergency arises I will be checking in once a day.

Fielding questions

One of the issues about navigating relationships and other connections is building community and managing expectations from both strangers and business clients.

As I pointed out in Lesson 1, when I share that I am living #LocationFree, the response is generally met with a screwed-up face and quizzical look, accompanied by a deluge of questions. These are some of my all-time favourites:

"Yes, but where do you *live*?"
"I don't have a fixed home."
"Yes, but where do you sleep?"
"In a bed."
"Yes, but where do your *really* live?"
Or, "Where is your home, Kate?"

Or a version of the following:
"Ooooooh! So you're homeless?"
"Mmm … so your business isn't doing well, is it?"

Or the opposite version:
"So I guess you're just trying to avoid tax?"
"Why don't you get a real job?"

"I guess you're single and have no responsibility?"

"You must have tons of money?"

"Your partner keeps you and supports you so that you can do all of this, right?"

"So you are just on permanent holiday?"

Answering and fielding questions or assumptions that come your way can be fun, and tell you much about the frame of mind of the other person. It tells you all about their view of the world, the prism or prison they may be trapped in.

One of my motivations behind writing this book was to inspire you to do the same. To leap into the unknown and try it – even if it's just for a year. Even if you keep all your stuff, and just pack it up and store it, rent out your home and go off on a jaunt to work #LocationFree – why the hell not? By the time you come back, everything will be just the way you left it. Or maybe you won't come back at all?

I know that in the last five years my lifestyle has already inspired people to think about it and do it for themselves. Simply because they have told me as much! The community living globally in this way is much larger than you think. I believe that, in the coming years and decades, more and more people are going to understand the idea of downsizing, minimising, reducing, recycling, reusing, living simpler, favouring experiences over stuff.

If you are feeling by a mixture of excitement and a little terror at the prospect, perhaps it is calling you to try it in the way you wish. I love hearing all the variations and permutations people come up with. It's why I interviewed all the others for this book – so that you get different voices, ideas and perspectives by hearing from men and women, married, single, divorced and parents for a more rounded viewpoint on this lifestyle.

Building community in a new location

Discussing settling in in Lesson 3, I suggested you find a local coffee shop as one of the ways to meet people and integrate. If you go to the same coffee shop at the same time every day, you will start encountering the same people. In this way, you can start connecting, or at the very least smiling and saying hello. You can share your passions with the owner or waiter and ask them to introduce you to locals they know.

I understand you might *never* do this in your own community back home, but think of it as a new way of looking at the world. I have always had the ability to strike up conversations with random people and have wonderful connections along the way – in queues, waiting at the bank, restaurants, grocery stores, at airports and even on transport. (I have to confess, though, that I generally speak *very* little on planes, simply because I don't always want to be stuck chatting to someone for 12 hours, and so I also know the art of the "gentle ignore".)

I am the same with animals … I go out of my way to pet, stroke and love cats and dogs wherever I can, with permission from the owner, of course. If it's a street cat or dog, I might have some treats to bribe a little love and attention from them. When spending a month in Argentina, I had a whole photo album dedicated to the beautiful street dogs of Bellville. When on the road I'll take four-pawed love any way I can get it. I also seem to be able to attract cats wherever I go!

How do you build community when you are brand new to a strange village, town or city? I just follow my passion and interest. But what are the things you love? And can you find similar-minded people already within a community? Finding just one person may mean connecting with many.

After the local coffee shop, local Facebook groups are my next "go-to". Ask around if there is a relevant local group and join up immediately – you can always exit when you move on. Chances are, just a simple search will lead you to local group. Are you a salsa dancer like me? If so, find the local club or a local class to tap into. If you love sailing, rock up at the local yacht club and introduce yourself. Or ask your worldwide community whether they know someone in the location you're headed to and are able to introduce you. You can even do that ahead of time. I have just done that for a dear friend.

A client who used to live in China employed me – without ever meeting me – to downsize and move his mum from a four-roomed house she had lived in for decades into a small two-room residence for the elderly. I met him only after I'd moved his mum. He now lives in Dubai and is an avid sailor. I recently saw that he had just done a leg of a worldwide race. At the same time, another dear friend was about to go and work in Dubai. He too sails and runs a marine business in the UK. So I had an idea … And *Bam!*, with one message I connected the two of them before my friend even got to Dubai! Want to know the real kicker? My client is a member of the one yacht club my friend had his eye on joining, but I did not know that. What are the chances?

Be bold and connect people with each other, and others will do the same for you. If you want to live this life really well, I suggest you get well versed in the art of asking for help, support and building community along the way. Connections can be also made locally and directly on the ground, or through your existing community connecting you to people they know there before you arrive.

Are you a member of an international organisation? YPO, Rotary, Community Chest, Internations, any professional bodies or hobby clubs? How easy is it to tap into those channels?

Do you love theatre? Make sure you book tickets the week you land so that you get the thrill of seeing something local that makes you feel alive and energised. Perhaps there's even a local theatre club.

Right now, as I wrap up the first draft of this book, I am in Malaga in southern Spain for the winter. I touched down in Spain for the first time seven weeks prior to run a Write 'n Walk retreat in Northern Asturias with my business partner. You see, for the two years since deciding that the USA was not where I wanted to settle with any permanence, Europe has been on my radar. I was already visiting Greece every year, but I also wanted to explore other countries in Europe to see where my next long-haul stopover could be. I came to explore Spain. I asked some folk where they thought I would enjoy staying for a few months, and they suggested Malaga. And that was it ... I arrived in Malaga having booked an apartment for six weeks. Soon after I arrived, I needed to move out because the apartment was way too noisy for me, and simultaneously secured a two-and-a-half-month housesit to the east of Malaga. I knew I wanted to write this very book – the one in your hands right now – as my winter project. So, in the interests of building community, I looked up the local Facebook groups for expats as well as online women's groups and co-working groups and got posting the following:

> *"Hola – I have just arrived in Malaga and am about to start writing my fifth book, and wondering if anyone wants to join me in writing. I don't care what you are writing, but let's meet up and do what I call BUMTIME."*

Within days, I had 25 people on a WhatsApp group, and that same week we had our first meeting. Instant community! It just takes a little courage. It was one of the easiest things to set up – so much so that a year later some of those folk are the very same ones you are reading about on these pages!

 **WHAT OTHERS SAY ABOUT ...**

Staying connected

There will always be birthdays, and maybe even weddings and funerals, that you miss. I like to spend Christmas with my family, so between South East Asia and Central America was one week in the Netherlands. And there were regular video calls and Facebook for photo sharing.

—André Gussekloo

I have always lived a very independent lifestyle and, because I worked in hospitality in my earlier years, I was often not present for these kinds of occasions anyway. My family and friends know that a gift may be given at a time other than the occasion date and the card may read, "Happy Xmas, Birthday, Easter, graduation, engagement and anything else I may have missed this year."

I am not a great long-distance communicator because I like to be immersed in the place I am in. As such, most of my loved ones know that we'll pick it up where we left off when we see each other again. My partner and I are intentional about our communication and we make time for each other when we are not together. For us, that does not mean daily check-ins but rather longer, more meaningful conversations once or twice a week.

—Lynne Scullard

Staying in touch with loved ones takes a bit of scheduling, depending on where you are in the world. Time zones are a factor to work with. Facebook messenger, WhatsApp and Skype are a few of the tools we use to get together with friends and family.

—Chris de Cap

I have become more aware of making memories, so when I go back home, if it's left to me to choose a venue to have lunch, I try to choose a place that not only suits the occasion, but that I know will remind us of the time spent together.

Missing milestones has been a particularly hard portion of this journey for me. However, I make sure that I remember those special occasions, and will return home with a gift that celebrates a missed anniversary, or birthday. This means I am shopping with purpose, remembering a friend or family member back home. It is an absolute joy to see their face when you finally do connect, and you can gift them something that you have bought months or weeks ago in a foreign place. It's a special token of your not being able to be there on the day, but still making sure they know you were there in spirit.

I also have set times that I make sure I am available to chat to my family back home. It's important that you stay connected, because life does move fast and time passes quickly, and before you know it, your level of communication can wane.

Be present! When I am home, I make sure I am not distracted by my phone or multitasking. I keep reminding myself of the times when I am away, missing the company of my family, so that when I am with them, I need to give them my full attention.

—Deborah Louise Botha

Phone. Phone. Phone. Apart from that, I am flexible with my time and decide where and when to go. Thus, for special celebrations, I can organise ahead of time.

—Nabila Welk

In terms of balancing my lifestyle with quality time, everywhere I travel I have friends so I'm always spending quality time with someone I love. And, yes, sure, I'll miss a lot of birthdays back in America and celebrations and holidays and whatnot, but I trade that for other birthdays, milestones and other celebrations. Because my circle of friends is so international, it doesn't matter where I am, I'm going to be missing some holiday or celebration somewhere in the world, but also gaining a celebration somewhere else. In terms of keeping in touch, I use WhatsApp and Facebook. However, a lot of my friendships are such that it doesn't matter how much time passes; when we do connect it'll be just like we were never apart, so the friendships don't really need a lot of time to maintain them.

—**Gene Ellis**

It can be hard not to be with family, especially when they celebrate birthdays etcetera, but modern technology is a wonderful thing. We speak regularly and keep in touch in a number of ways as each family member seems to prefer a different app, from Messenger to WhatsApp, Skype to Zoom, email and text! My two kids and I surprised my dad with a group WhatsApp video call on his eightieth birthday. I always know what my younger generation family is up to from Facebook and Instagram, whilst I share my photos and updates so they can see where we are and what we're doing.

Rob's mum, in her nineties, isn't computer literate so we bought a small photo printer to print out our pics and post back to her, whilst her grandchildren use a tablet to show her our Facebook photos. She didn't understand our choice and worried about our lifestyle and not having a settled home, so seeing photos of us being happy and all the great scenery, backed up by regular phone calls, reassured her a little. The rest of our family understand and, despite missing us, encouraged us to go for it!

Family have visited us for a cheap holiday in the sun, but due to living short-term in properties, it has been impossible to find a pet sitter (and we'd never consider kennels) so Rob and I travel back to the UK separately.

I think it's imperative for us to take the initiative when maintaining contact with family and friends. We chose to "leave" them, so I feel a responsibility to frequently check in by sending messages or picking up the phone.

—Nancy Benn

Again, I'm in NYC six-plus months, so not so much an issue. I use WhatsApp, Facebook and Facetime.

—Uday Jhunjhunwala

I make sure I carve out time each week to speak with family and friends back in the UK. I use WhatsApp to stay connected. I always try to travel home for specific celebrations. I'm lucky that I am only a short flight away so that is a help and was a key part of the decision-making process when I was looking at where I wanted to be based.

—Victoria Jane Watson

I have a Messenger group with my closest friends and we share everything there. I normally also make friends wherever I go, so I never feel lonely. I love deep people and it's not difficult to find other like-minded people when you're deep. I have next to no family and what little I have, we have nothing in common.

—Mette Glargaard

Not so well, sadly. My immediate family, we are of gypsy blood, I guess. Two years after I left South Africa, my parents left too and they went to New Zealand where my stepfather has a son. So they're in New Zealand,

194 | 10 Lessons for Living #LocationFree

my sister lives in Hong Kong, I have several stepbrothers, and they live in Canada, South Africa, dotted all over. We're not as close as I would love us to be. Social media is a gift because it gives my mother and I insight in each other's lives, so that's a joy. We Skype, of course, or Facetime, but I do miss those occasions.

Friends I find easier to make because – well, it depends again which country you're in ... Expatriates generally hold each other dear because they become each other's family. So I have some friendships here that were made within three hours because, hey, I'm an expat and you're an expat and so let's be best friends and we will have each other's backs if anything goes wrong. Older expats are wonderful – they go, "Oh shame, you're here with no family! Become our family. Come to our family home for Christmas."

And also the expat community moves and that's very sad because you make friends with somebody for two years and then they are reposted somewhere or they're moving back to their home country. So it's been quite difficult for me to learn that your friends are going to move, leave and change. Social media is again a blessing for that because you make friends with somebody and they leave, but you retain the friendship virtually and in a social space. So that's nice.

This year I chose not to celebrate my birthday. Actually, it's quite common. I regularly choose not to celebrate my birthday because it's on New Year's Eve and it's awkward. I'm not a big fussed person about my own birthday so it doesn't bother me at all. It was my sister's birthday too. We share the same day and I miss being with her because that's special ... But the older I get, these things become less important. Like my own birthday becomes less important and I'm of an age where I'm not really being invited to my friends' weddings any more because we're past that.

—**Michelle Clarke**

I travel between two countries quite often, so I see my friends and relatives every three to five months. While I'm gone we stay in touch by WhatsApp, Messenger or Facebook and we often plan in advance what we are going to do when we see each other again. My transitions between countries are usually quite well planned so it's quite easy to match calendars. When I'm travelling through a country, I try to make a long relay or stopover to see a friend in London or Barcelona, or to have coffee at the airport with a friend in Amsterdam while waiting for my connection. I sometimes also travel to meet people, or they come meet me.

Having children doesn't mean you can't travel or live location independent, but its different kind of life. You can't expect children to adapt to it all and just go with the flow. Some do, many don't. If you have children, you should get a home base and travel shorter trips. It's also very stressful to be on the road, work several hours per day and entertain the kids 24/7 at the same time. Most families who work and travel full time have just one working parent and the other one is dedicated to the needs of the children. A single parent or two working parents will have it easier living mostly steady and taking holidays for travelling - in other words, not working when travelling. The children get most out of your lifestyle choice if they are able to learn the local language and make local/international friends. Putting children in a local school is a great way to make them feel at home, though it may take some time for them to settle. It's easier to travel or move with younger children than teenagers, unless the teen really wants to go see the world and is willing to leave his/her friends. Teens have a hard time adapting to new places if they didn't vote for moving.

—Katia Enbuske

I'm lucky that I can say yes or no to jobs that come in. I can "block out" any special occasions in my diary and work around them. I haven't missed anything significant yet! My top tip for staying connected is with groups; Facebook Messenger, WhatsApp, Loomio - whatever works for each community I'm connected to. Through these groups, we share everyday things; it's not just about my international travel - it's about my daughter's cat or dog, about the funny man my son met on a train station, how the organisation is running, what documents I need to pay attention to, how urgent is the email that was sent ... Keeping it normal and everyday is important so I'm not "checking in" on them all. It's just part of my daily life ... I've also become very good at mediating sibling rivalry through Facebook Messenger! Haha!

I tend to see my children more often now than when I was living at home and travelling a lot for work because my travel to them is now more intentional. It is quality time of a few days instead of a rushed weekend!

Then the other thing is, if I have the opportunity to say yes or take up some work that is near them, I make sure I've got an extra couple of days either side so that I can go and stay with my children and really catch up.

Then things like my mother whose husband passed away about 18 months ago and I don't get near her region often, so I have to be very intentional about that. So I make sure that I go and stay with her for a week to spend some good time with her. Once when I got back from Chicago I was exhausted and I just wanted to stop, but I got a hire car and drove six hours straight to my mum's and I stayed there for five days just to make sure I saw her before Christmas.

There was one time I landed from Europe in Sydney airport and I knew I just had to ring my mum. I rang her and as soon as I heard her voice and went, "Yep, okay. Everything's good. Good, good, good," and hung up, I kind of looked around at the flights again and went, "All right, I'm ready to leave again." I just needed to land and hear her voice and that *was okay. So, yeah, all the online platforms like Zoom and the Facebook groups and all of that keep me very well connected. I just make sure I'm really intentional about it.*

—Dee Brooks

I go for walks and speak on the phone to check in with people. I try to "take them with me" when I walk so they know the area I'm in so it's like they're there. I'm super aware of being present when I speak to my loved ones too. It's important to create that space and not get too distant.

I'm fortunate to only be three hours from my family and I'm able to jump on a flight if necessary. When I do see my loved ones, I'm there 100%. I plan my travel around the holidays and invite people over as much as possible.

—Carolynne Alexander

That's a difficulty for some people. I can imagine!

For me, days like birthdays, name days or whatever are not important. I'm in good contact by phone and WhatsApp with my family and friends. I love to enjoy the celebrations in the places where I am.

—Jan van Kuijk

 **TOP TIPS!**

- Strike a balance between building a new local community and connecting to your support system back "home".
- Keep kindness and compassion as your compass.
- Living #LocationFree is a crash course in understanding yourself and other human beings – relish the lessons it offers.

If I was just starting out

IF I WAS JUST STARTING out again today, in truth, there is nothing I would do differently. I don't mean that arrogantly – just that I am entirely at peace with my choices along the way, even the supposed crappy ones.

I am deeply aware I have missed out on some very important events of loved ones: deaths, marriages, births, milestone anniversaries, house moves, business awards, birthdays and so much more. Nothing can ever replace being there in the flesh, but my beloveds also know me and can feel my presence in a different way. My job is to be me – fully me. To embrace that in taking up my rightful place in the world.

The flip side is that I get to celebrate incredible times with the people I am with in the country at the time. The sheer delight of travel, cultures and friendships that deepen rapidly in this global community. A shared glass of wine or a hike with a brand-new friend can elicit the most vulnerable of conversations, because there is nothing to lose by diving in, each of you as vulnerable as the other. I have also experienced such joy in sharing exciting new destinations with family, partner and friends when they are lured to visit.

I have made peace with the fact that not everyone understands, likes or respects my lifestyle but, at the end of the day, what other people think is their business, isn't it?

It is hard to believe that what started out as an idea to downsize, pack up and live #LocationFree for just one year has now morphed into five years. Travelling and living this lifestyle has forever changed me. Even though I was always a minimalist in nature, I realise at an even deeper level now just how little we truly need to live the most glorious life. A life that matters and impacts the world positively. In this time, I have learned:

- that experience trumps all things,
- to choose memories over mementoes, and
- to do more and be more.

I have found it heartwarming, invigorating and humbling travelling this way for five years. The most significant factor to be cognisant of, in my opinion, is to stay strong, healthy, safe and truly connected to your heart and values. Immerse yourself in the community you choose to visit or live in and take proper care of your clients, business or work. Listen to the rumblings of your heart and stay bold, curious and open.

Try your best to do no harm and be respectful of cultures in which you travel. Contribute time, energy and money into the local communities in which you choose to live. Slow down, immerse and revel in your brave choices.

This lifestyle epitomises the notion of *Tread lightly*. All the #LocationFree people and communities with whom I have connected are super professional, a heady mix of work and play hard, are conscious and mindful of the impact they have and the footprint they leave. After all, #LocationFree simply implies living with less stuff, consuming less, buying less and needing less. Fewer worldly possessions and more life obsessions.

We are constantly exposed to different cultures, ideas, food and, in this increasingly global village, it feels like I am an integral part of life on this earth. I love being exposed to new ideas and different customs, hearing different languages fall on my ears as I try to get my tongue around the language.

I love soaking up the sheer beauty of this planet. Whether you choose to move often and fast, or prefer to stay longer and immerse in the slow lane, you get to figure it all out. I hope that by sharing some of my story and all the generous insights from the other brave souls interviewed, we have helped you take the leap.

No matter what challenges the world is throwing at us all – economic, political, religious, climatic and, of course, global health crises – there will always be personal choices to make. How do we navigate the ebb and flow and will we use external circumstances as an excuse to stay put, play it safe and say no, or will we use those very same issues as motivation to *just do it*?

Want a laugh? After five years of summer and "shoulder seasons", it is somewhat ironic – and challenging – to think I willingly chose to spend winter in Scotland. *Brrrrrr!* After four months of lockdown with family in the UK, I ventured to the wee remote island of Iona off the west coast of Scotland. I refer to that personal retreat time as "Honouring the Call Of Closure" and you can read an in-depth blog on my website about it. After Iona, I needed somewhere to spend the rest of winter finishing this book and learning the art of book binding – my new hobby!

I am filled with deep gratitude that I have managed to spend most of the past five years in warmer climates, with lashings of Vitamin D, long swims and sunny days that stretch into forever. So having to go and buy thermals, gloves and a hat was a bit of a shock to my system!

Change is afoot and, as I write this, I am creating the next iteration of #LocationFree. I am considering a little less travel, fewer flights, fewer countries. Perhaps shifting between worldwide travel and a base that will keep me in one place for two thirds of the year, welcoming others on their global gallivants. My next evolution will be revealed as I live into it. Maybe you will come and hang out with me on retreat in an exotic location?

I hope that we have answered most of your questions, that some wild ideas have been sparked and taken root in your heart. That at least some of your fears have been allayed, wiped away, as we helped you shift and ease into some possible ideas.

Have we inspired you to listen to the yearning in your heart? How are *you* going to embark on your own version of a curated life well lived?

Go Lightly
Kate
kate-emmerson.com

 **WHAT OTHERS SAY ABOUT ...**

Starting out

I wish I started doing this earlier. I thought I needed to be in one place in order to find a lasting relationship (still hasn't happened) and so I was reluctant to travel a lot. Even loneliness will pass and sometimes surprise you. Just do it. Explore the world whenever you can. There are so many beautiful places and experiences to be had.

—*Uday Jhunjhunwala*

Dive in and do it sooner. Be prepared for the low times as well as the good. Be your own best friend and travel more!

—**Carolynne Alexander**

If I were just starting out, I would say to myself, "Hey, you're about to really push yourself out of your comfort zones and grow in a lot of ways and it's going to be a really great thing." I feel as though the challenges that have arisen from a lot of international travel have done nothing but contribute to me growing a lot as a person. So, yeah, I would just tell myself to be ready to have the trip of a lifetime and to really embrace the journey while you're able to.

One disturbing trend that I have been observing is that remote work is becoming more and more popular, which is great. However, a lot of the pioneers of early remote work, in my opinion, were Digital Nomads running their own business. So they were location independent because they were running their own businesses and starting their own projects and I think that's great. With the explosion of remote work and a lot more people wanting to do it, people are asking the wrong questions such as - and I see these posts every day - "Hey, I want to work remotely. Where's the best place to find a job?" And so what's happening is that a lot of people, because they're so attracted to the remote lifestyle, are basically replacing a job from home they don't really want to do with just a job online that they don't really want to do. That's not really the spirit of remote work, which is working on a passion, monetising it and experiencing the full enjoyment of work and play merging together. If you're just going to replace the job you don't like with any online job you don't like then there's no point. You're just not going to be happy.

—**Gene Ellis**

You connect with more people by staying in hostels instead of Airbnbs and get insider tips on the situation and what to see from other travellers. If

204 | 10 Lessons for Living #LocationFree

you want to try out this lifestyle, you can pack a carry-on and travel your own country or a neighbouring country for a month, live in hostels and see what it's like. Even if you don't like it, you'll learn something about yourself.

—**Mette Glargaard**

Let's Go Do This! I wish I had started earlier and been braver sooner in my life.

There are many reasons we choose not to live on the edge of our comfort zones and spaces. We have been conditioned to believe that unknown waters are dangerous and damming. My experience has been quite the opposite. Life on the edge has many hidden pitfalls and stumbles over rocky pathways, but when you get to see the view from the edge of comfort, it truly is magnificent! Be Brave – You are Worth It!

—**Deborah Louise Botha**

You are doing the right thing!

We've had to travel on a budget and it's frustrating that housing has been so expensive. We love our pets, hence bringing them along, but our journey would have been a little easier without dogs.

I had looked at pet-sitting options, but no one wanted a pet sitter who brought their own pets along! I looked into Workaway availabilities, but most accommodation was shared with the host. One of our dogs is a nervy barker; this would have been most stressful. Due to our budget, some homes have been rustic with uncomfortable sagging sofas, ill-equipped kitchens or erratic electricity, etcetera, but this has been part of the adventure! We honestly haven't missed having our own possessions or anything that we left behind in England, nor have we regretted our decision. We do have some fantastic memories of our experiences, backed up by photo evidence, that money just cannot buy!

—**Nancy Benn**

Luckily, I heard this saying in my early days: "The traveller sees what he sees, the tourist sees what he has come to see." My preference is always a traveller. Have two to three "must-see" options on your list and then let go. Be free. Plans will always go the way they want, not the way you want. Learn to be flexible and aware. When it rains on the day you were supposed to be in the sun, find the beauty. Smile.

—**Lynne Scullard**

If I could tell myself something that would be really useful to start the journey it's to start making digital art right away. Get rid of most of those physical art supplies, but keep the paintbrushes. It's just too much clutter to travel with. Another thing would be: don't go to another country without your tattoo equipment.

—**Chris de Cap**

Don't bring your cat – it slows you down!

—**André Gussekloo**

Get focused and write down what you want out of the experience of location independent. Planning is key and I think it's important to work out how you're going to switch up your lifestyle and what your goals are as a starting point. Running a business and travelling is not the easiest thing to do and creating a sustainable plan to allow you to do both is imperative.

—**Victoria Jane Watson**

To be honest, I would not do a lot different. I would say: Go for it!

I was lucky enough that my whole body, mind and heart were shouting at me to get out of my "old life", so I didn't have any doubts about jumping into the deep end, selling my house and quitting my job.

Whatever you do, listen to your heart and you can never go wrong.

—Martin van den Berg

I'd say I did it the right way and I would do it the same again.

Respect the locals and their culture wherever you go. Learn the local language, at least to some extent, be polite, respect local social codes, smile, be patient, don't get upset if things don't run the way you're used to in your home country. Bear in mind also that everything usually goes much smoother when you make an effort: if you speak the local language and know how to behave, you don't get cheated, ignored or treated the same way as those who are perceived as expats and tourists. In a lot of places locals don't like certain foreigners and they usually have a reason for it. Don't pay over price for products, accommodation or services; don't leave crazy tips. If you think you're "helping" the locals by throwing around money, you're actually doing the opposite: you're spoiling the local economy and soon the locals can't afford to live in their own city.

—Katia Enbuske

Do exactly the same as you did! Enjoy all you are doing and realise every second you are a blessed person - you can visit every beautiful place on this earth.

—Jan van Kuijk

I think people believe that to travel is expensive. I have discovered and learned that to settle and root down is more expensive than to travel. If people are thinking about that in terms of "I can't afford to have a lifestyle that includes so much moving around", I disagree. It is affordable. It teaches you to live more affordably so you become smarter and wiser with how you spend and how you do. So, if finance is a concern to somebody,

I'd say, "Go out there. Try it and give yourself several months and then do your calculations and determine whether that was an expensive or an inexpensive alternate choice."

I wish I had started earlier in my application for my Visa Permanencia here in Chile. I stalled that process because I was, "Am I staying, am I going? Am I staying, am I going?" It cost me money in the end and cost me time. When I saw that there was an opportunity, and I saw that quite early on, I wish I'd acted on it. I saw it and I thought, "Oh, nice opportunity," and I kind of left it there to think about. And it took me two or three years before I said, "I must take that opportunity."

I think we do well to give ourselves as many opportunities for a global living arrangement. So, for example, I'm a resident of South Africa, but now I have a visa in Chile, I have an opportunity for a second base for assets, for work, for contacts. If I were to move to another country and they were to offer me a visa too, I could have a third base. I think I'm liking the idea of diversifying like that. So I think that when one sees that there are opportunities, one should put in the effort, do the research and do that because we're living in a world that is unstable and so to have some options globally, I think, is a good choice.

—Michelle Clarke

Being a Digital Nomad isn't only the glamorous Instagram life. As long as you haven't been retired and have to work for a living, you need to be able to focus and to learn how to develop a routine for your work, otherwise you might fail badly. And not to forget that you have to deal with lots of different people and situations when travelling; thus, if you are slow in adapting and don't like changes, it might be a huge challenge for you.

—Nabila Welk

If I was starting out on this path today I would rethink my luggage, consider what I really needed and eliminate what is not useful and that it's all just "stuff" - anything can be replaced.

I'd tell myself that there are good people in the world to learn from and travel with, and that trust is just as important as following your gut instinct about safety and make sure you let someone know where in the world you are.

I would tell myself to let all my loved ones know that they should not buy me gifts, not even "flat" presents! The first year, good-intentioned friends bought me "flat" things that could go into my suitcase and I ended up with a six-inch pile of "flat presents" that I had to leave at my sister's place; it all adds up.

I would also tell myself to reach out to someone when I'm feeling down; don't expect people to just know how you're feeling - they see you online having a wonderful international adventure and could easily think everything is okay; don't expect them to know - reach out when needed! Stop, pause, reflect and act.

—Dee Brooks

 **TOP TIPS!**

- Talk to others, but trust your gut. You are the one who knows you best.
- Take that leap – you can change your mind as you navigate it all.
- Say yes to the sheer adventure of it all, but don't second-guess your heart when it says no.

LESSON

10

#LocationFree hacks, tips and resources

A LONG THE WAY, I HAVE found some very useful tools, apps and what we now call #hacks. I thought it would be useful to put some of our joint favourite tips together for you. I hope you find one or two to support your journey.

Health aps

- **Yoga:** Down Dog has an awesome free version.
- **Meditation:** Choose from Calm, Headspace, Insight Timer and Mindvalley, for instance. Pick one and get into it, and if you use it extensively then consider paying for the service. Deepak Chopra and Oprah regularly offer free 21-day meditation courses throughout the year

International networks

Are you part of a bigger global organisation for business, a particular hobby or charity that you can tap into when living #LocationFree?

- **Internations:** For expats with local chapters in different countries. Free sign-in membership and you can upgrade to paid version as required.
- **Facebook groups:** Local Facebook groups in your city are a gold mine for connecting in a new space.
- **Global Nomad** or **Digital Nomad websites:** Look for country-specific ones: https://www.coworker.com/

Financial apps

- Add all your personal banking apps, such as HSBC and Santander.
- **2FA:** I use Two Factor Authentification for better security.
- **Transferwise:** International currency billing and payments.
- **PayPal:** easy when on the move
- **Luno or Altcointrader:** Use for crypto currencies.
- **Xero:** Accounting
- **Receipt Bank:** Accounting
- **XE:** Real-time currency converter.
- **LastPass:** This is a brilliant way to digitally store your entire password in one "vault". This changed my life three years ago because having my password written down in some form was definitely not safe and wasted so much time trying to retrieve them. Worth every penny that you pay for it!
- **Payfast** and **Stripe:** Certain websites use different interfaces for payments between shopping carts and your bank.

Accommodation

- **Travel Wallet:** All accommodation, boarding passes, tickets and bookings stored in one clever app.

- **Airbnb:** A wonderful way to find local accommodation of all quality and prices – from a room in someone's home to luxury apartments across the world. The platform also offers certain guarantees and recourse should something go wrong.
- **Booking.com:** Hotels, studios and apartments – the more you use it the better your reward status and discounts.
- **Couchsurfing Travel:** You might even get a bed instead of a couch with this network of people who love meeting folk and welcoming you into their home. Not just for youngsters.
- **Local accommodation**: What works best will depend on where you are. For example, Spain uses **Idealista** as an accommodation platform. Scotland uses **Spare Room**. Stay updated via local groups as to what everyone is using in each area. Some are better than others!
- **Co-living spaces:** Connect with local Digital Nomad and co-work spaces at your destination ahead of time to pre-build a network.
- **Trustedhousesitters.com** and **Housecarers.com:** For international house- and pet sitting-opportunities.

Communication

- **Google Translate:** Communicate in a foreign language – great for directions, local greetings and important information.
- **Language schools:** If you are travelling to a country where the dominant language is not your own, why not book into a language school for the first two weeks? Start brushing up your language skills immediately and get to know the local community by having to get to class every day; often, the classes are filled with expats of all ages from all over the world. They often have social activities and day trips, which may help you connect with others really fast.
- **Local "Guide to":** When in a new city or location, ask around or Google to check whether there is a local *Guide to*

XYZ. These are usually packed with info on current events, and will always point you to interesting places, people and shops. If you are staying for a couple of months, be sure to sign up to their newsletter so that you stay up to date with everything that's happening in your location.

- **Meet up:** This is a great way to connect with like-minded folk for business and pleasure. Look out for all the local events, wine tastings, expat meet-ups and business networking opportunities in your area.
- **Language**: Try DuoLingo, Rosetta Stone and Babbel.

Staying connected

- **Skype:** Calls and live video on your phone and computer.
- **Zoom:** More stable than Skype and my personal preference and the tool I used for many years for all my online coaching and groups. There is a free version to start off with, or upgrade to the paid facility for more functionality. In 2020, the entire world became more Zoom friendly!
- **WhatsApp**: Perfect for messages, voice messages and video calls, it will be available on your phone, with some functionality on your computer. Great on local wifi.
- **Facebook:** For video calls and messages. Great on local wifi.
- **Marco Polo:** This facility combines text, social media and video chats in one! Works a little like WhatsApp and the recipient can download the message when they get it in their time zone.
- **Bonjoro:** A really fun video app.
- **Slack** or **Monday.com:** Great apps for phone and computer – similar to Facebook if you want to run groups, and takes a little time to get into how to maximize it.
- **Viber:** Great for group video calls and works better in some countries than others.

Documents and technology management

- **Google Docs:** A cloud-based way in which documents and spreadsheets can be created, edited and stored online. Great for sharing with family, teams or clients on the go.
- **Dropbox:** Another cloud-based option for sharing documents, files and images.
- **Team Viewer:** This enables password-protected third-party access to your computer. It has saved me many times when my computer played up and no one could fix it (the joy of being on remote islands and the closest Apple store is a 90-minute car trip plus an hour's flight to the mainland).
- **Evernote:** Wonderful app that synchs with both computer and phone – a great way to compartmentalise your thoughts and notes.
- **SignEasy** (or equivalent): Sign documents when you can't print them off. Not all legal documents will accept digital signatures, but can get you out of sticky situations.
- **CamScanner** (or equivalent): Scan physical documents to send off to a third party when a photograph just won't cut it.

Getting around

- **Google Maps**: Generally, the instinctive go-to option when looking up destinations and other locations – but be sure to have data on your phone or a handy wifi spot close by.
- **maps.me:** An amazing app by which to download maps of areas to use on your phone when you have no wifi or connectivity. Especially handy when in a foreign country and not yet on wifi or have a local sim card for connectivity.
- **Uber:** Usually a little cheaper than local taxis, and can order via the app and pay with a credit card. You don't need cash – just pre-register payment details on your phone.
- **Local taxi app**: Helpful to have on phone as a back up to Uber.

- **Lyft:** Some cities have this facility, which is very handy for sharing cheaper rides.
- **Moovit** (bus and train): Most countries have local bus and train apps, and some might even have location-specific ones for that city.

Insurance

Insurance is very country dependent, so shop around and ask your community for what works best. Sometimes you can extend your existing health insurance for travel. Some companies offer limited insurance when paying by credit card for flights. Try Cigna Global (that's my provider) and Bupa for health options, and travelinsurance.com for international travel.

Inspirational ideas

- **Podcasts:** Always load your favourite ones for regular pick-me-ups.
- **TED Talks:** Little zaps of energy of usually no longer than 12 or 18 minutes. Great for when a slump hits and you need a pick-me-up fast.
- **Audible.com** (audio books): I love listening to audio books when travelling. I also keep an Evernote list of books and audio books as I come across them. The next time I'm on Audible or in an actual bookstore, I just open up that list to see which one I should grab next.

Social media

You probably know all of these, but these are some fun apps.
- **Instagram Layout:** Create collage pictures.
- **Prisma:** Alter the look and feel of your pics using template themes.
- **Snapseed:** Add text, vignettes and frames, and edit pics.
- **Foodie:** Enhances all pics, not just food images.

WHAT OTHERS SAY ABOUT ...

Resources and other tips

Nomad List is a good resource just for staying up to date on nomad-based news in terms of places to go and whatnot. Spotify is probably the most used app just to have some music. For iPhone users, I have the AirPods Pro headphones – great quality with noise cancellation built in, so great for flying. I definitely suggest noise-cancellation headphones. That way if you're flying, travelling or simply working, you can block out the background noise.

Airbnb is great – I use that a lot to book a week before you get somewhere and then book longer term after you've stayed in town. Facebook is really great for finding apartments; one trick that I do is to add myself to a bunch of groups and then I access the Facebook marketplace and I've noticed that it aggregates all the things for sale and for rent in my groups into one place. Nice little trick that not a lot of people know about.

—*Gene Ellis*

Google the weather because it's important to know that to expect when in a foreign place.

Duolingo: it's always nice to at least greet local people - it also enriches your travel experience and people just want to help you when you have taken the time to greet them in their native language. My all-time favourite gadget is the collapsible/folding kettle I bought off Amazon.

—**Deborah Louise Botha**

Google Maps. We bought a Satnav for our travels, but it couldn't find some addresses that Google could. I've also identified places to visit by searching Maps for photos and reviews that users have posted and also contribute myself.

Google Translate. I use this on my phone when out and about and PC for translating websites, documents or writing emails.

TripAdvisor. To find things to do, places to visit and read the reviews for all. I also add reviews and photos of my own.

—Nancy Benn

Apart from my MacBook Air, Bose blue-tooth speaker, AirPods, and Kindle, which are such great travel companions, apps are my most used resources.

TripIt: I like keeping my trip itineraries in one place and what I love about this app is that it tracks the distances I've travelled and what my carbon footprint is that I can offset against.

—Lynne Scullard

Before going to a new country, I recommend downloading the app maps. me and downloading the maps of the country. Google Maps fails to provide accurate information. For example, in Morocco, maps.me will accurately show you every nook and cranny of each of the medinas in the cities. Google Maps shows dead ends when there are tunnels, while maps.me shows you what's actually there.

However, maps.me relies on travellers' input for its details, and sometimes doesn't show store fronts and other businesses. So if you go to a nice restaurant or a cool art gallery, mark it in maps.me and share it. That way, others can find these wonderful things. So this is where Google Maps is better, but it still might not set you on a good route.

One great tip if you are in an area without wifi and need to communicate is that Facebook messenger uses the least amount of data compared to many other apps. While WhatsApp is one of the highest data eaters.

We use www.skyscanner.com to find great deals on flights. We also have profiles on www.workaway.info and www.housecarers.com, which help us with the work exchange and housesitting gigs.

—*Chris de Cap*

Lonely Planet for first impressions of a destination.

Tropical MBA podcast for latest Digital Nomad news, destination, business opportunities.

Dynamite Circle: a paid forum for successful online entrepreneurs.

Coworker.com: a directory of co-working spaces around the world.

NomadList: a constantly changing ranking of destinations by climate, internet speed, cost of living, etcetera.

Fun video for packing: youtube.com/watch?v=qjKybGvXFYo

—*André Gussekloo*

Facebook for randomly finding out if someone is in the same place. White Noise for improved sleep.

—*Uday Jhunjhunwala*

My main tip would be: don't just react to the outside world, but make time to connect to what happens on the inside as well. My way of doing this is meditation, which I can't emphasise enough is so important to do, but I am sure there are loads of different ways to stop and listen to yourself if meditation is not your thing: go fishing, hiking, rowing or whatever, without distracting yourself with music, mobile phones or anything else that is keeping you from listening to within. And why I love it is simply because it keeps me (slightly) sane and grounded. Without mediation, I quickly become much more susceptible to outside influences, opinions, etcetera.

If you find places on your travels that make your heart smile, make sure to return to them once in a while, especially when you are going through hard times. They will be the places that recharge your battery. For me this would be a Buddhist centre in Ireland (Dzogchen Beara) and a donkey sanctuary in the north of Spain (http://www.paraisodelburro.org), both of which I return to regularly to work as a volunteer. Why? Just re-read the first line of this paragraph ...

Wherever you are, make the effort to learn a few words in the local language, enough to allow you to say hello and order a beer or a coffee, for example. You making this effort will, in turn, mean that the locals make much more of an effort to understand you and do their best to help you. Why? Not only will you get things done much easier, but you'll be making people happy, and be on the receiving end of a lot more smiles instead of grumpiness.

Personally, I find pleasure/happiness in being able to fix most things I have with me, like my backpack, clothes and laptop. Which is a great resource in itself, being able to do that. So I carry a repair kit with the essentials like needle and thread, some rope, and some spare items, like a belt buckle, for instance.

—Martin van den Berg

A tip is to learn just the basics of any language in a given country – that will make your stay a lot better. Learn to travel only with your carry-on. It makes life so much easier to not carry a lot of luggage.

Check Meetup and Couchsurfing when getting to a new place to connect with people. Check if there's a Facebook group for people in that area, locals or foreigners, so you can easily get into the community.

Learn to say no and stick to it. You'll need it!

—**Mette Glargaard**

If you want this life style:

- *Plan ahead.*
- *Make sure the job you're doing is solid or, if you're starting your own business, make sure it's running well before you embark on your journey.*
- *If you're in customer service, it's better to travel in similar time zones where your customers are otherwise you will be working unpleasant hours.*
- *Leave room for life: if you have to work eight hours per day, it is difficult to combine with travelling and enjoying life.*
- *Familiarise yourself with the working conditions before you go to a new place: ask other Digital Nomads about practicalities like internet connections and costs, about co-working spaces, where to find likeminded people.*

—**Katia Enbuske**

The best I did was working and thinking long about my technical infrastructure for internet, calling, being called, data storage, cloud storage, backup – and avoiding of single point of failure situations.

I'm starting to explain all on my own website and, in the future, in my book.

—***Jan van Kuijk***

Some apps are country dependent. I've been using this fabulous, fabulous tool called Omio in Europe, which searches for buses, planes, trains, the cheapest routes between places and that, just in Europe, is the most delicious product. It doesn't work here in Latin America.

And the other tool I really, really like is TripIt. I'm a great fan of TripIt. I'm going to Patagonia next month and I send my Airbnb plans to TripIt and I send my air flight plan and then TripIt sends me a note and it says, "Hey, you haven't booked your flight home. Why don't you do that now?" And then I say, "No, actually, I have. And here's the flight number." And it finds all the details and plugs me in. And so it's really a super, super app.

When I was in Kuala Lumpur, as I boarded the airplane, I was given a gift called an Flexiroam X, and it has saved me a thousand times. It's an international roaming sim card and I can tell it which country I'm in, tell it I want to buy local data and it purchases me local data. Or I can tell it I'm not sure which countries I'm going to be in, can I buy global data? And it buys me global data.

So I always have data. If I don't, sometimes I forget to top up, or I'm using more than I thought I was and I land up on the top of a hill and I ask Google Maps where I am and it tells me you're nowhere – it can't find me because I have no data, then I'll do the run for the closest coffee shop. Anything that has a sign on it that says wifi. I'll go to that place and I'll buy myself a coffee, tap into their wifi and upload some data on my Flexiroam.

—Michelle Clarke

Compartmentalise everything! Everything has its place; there is no room for haphazard packing. All sections of my luggage are for particular pieces and I can notice very easily if something is missing.

Be ready for any adventures or changes; I have three bathroom bags, one small one in my handbag that could get me through one night without my luggage, one medium-sized one in my laptop bag for weekends away from my main luggage, and one main large one, which stays in my suitcase. Each one has different-sized shampoo, soaps, toothbrushes, tablets, deodorants, etcetera.

I have a sentence that goes through my head before I walk out any door for the final time: "Wallet, water, passport, chargers." With these four things checked, I can mentally go through each of my three pieces of luggage and tick everything off – I've never lost anything yet!

Always make sure someone knows where you are! I once arrived in Indonesia and realised that no one knew the address of where I was heading to and I quickly emailed my friend and colleague.

Always keep a change of clothes in your carry-on luggage. I have had one experience of my luggage not turning up and it was good to be able to go straight to my hotel and shower and change into clean clothes until my luggage arrived.

Talk to locals about places to visit or see; don't rely on tourist information if you want to see the real life of a place. I have been invited to people's homes for meals and seen areas of the world that I never would have seen on the tourist trail.

—Dee Brooks

Start connecting around the world

Gene Ellis

Location-independent entrepreneur travelling the world with insatiable curiosity and fascination. Simultaneously utilising all available technology to create scalable businesses to uplift and be in the service of others.

https://www.linkedin.com/in/genelamarellis/
"One life, best life."

Nancy Benn

Nancy Benn is a versatile virtual assistant with more than 10 years' experience providing efficient support to clients. Working remotely from her home office, Nancy helps entrepreneurs achieve more time and headspace to develop their business by supporting and encouraging their endeavours by providing outstanding, skilled admin and secretarial support.

www.directpaservices.co.uk
www.nancybenn.com
"Accept every opportunity and work out the details later."

Nabila Welk

Natural-born healer and spiritual guide, ex-dancer, body worker (yoga, Tai Chi, Rückenschule), business builder, and certified therapist and instructor with a focus on Eastern therapies such as Tibetan medicine, Daoist teaching, traditional Japanese Reiki, Thai medicine and nutrition.

www.NabilaWelk.com
www.facebook.com/NabilaWelk
"Live as if you were to die tomorrow – Learn as if you were to live forever."

Lynne Scullard

I'm living a fabulous, full life. I find business opportunities where there are social problems and turn them into profitable opportunities that make a tangible difference. I love my work, I love to travel and I love making a positive contribution. I also love finding reasons to celebrate. There are many.

https://www.linkedin.com/in/lynne-scullard-b708137/
http://beunsettled.co/
"Every day we get to make a choice about how we show up. Fill your own cup so that you can share with others abundantly. Leave space for the magic to appear. For if life is not joyous then what is the point?"

Chris de Cap

I've been an artist my whole life, more than half of which as a tattoo artist. I spent the bulk of my adult life being nomadic, however, mostly in Canada. Now I've taken my nomadic habits out into the world.

www.instagram.com/artisticvoyages

www.artisticvoyages.com
"There's one thing I've lived by in my life that will probably not change, and that is: don't f**king worry about shit."

Andre Gussekloo

André Gussekloo is fascinated by travel, entrepreneurship, and the internet. He has combined these interests to live the Digital Nomad lifestyle. As an author, André's goal is to inspire people to live extraordinary lives.

www.andregussekloo.com
"Live your dream."

Uday Jhunjhunwala

I am a fiction writer, filmmaker and investor, living in NYC, hoping the Dodgers move back to Brooklyn one day.

https://medium.com/@uday73
https://twitter.com/uday73
"If not now, when?"

Victoria Jane Watson

Victoria is a business and media mentor working with female entrepreneurs leading the way in the health and wellness industry. She gets to the heart of what makes her clients unique, showing them how to leverage their story and expertise effectively so they can build a personal brand that supports their business goals.

www.victoriajanewatson.com
Instagram: @victoriajanewatson
"Feel the fear and do it anyway!"

Martin van den Berg

Professional full-time housesitter, capable with all animals but specialising in big or "difficult" dogs and packs. Willing to travel.

dutch.mountainman@gmail.com
https://www.facebook.com/martinvdberg73
"Do what makes you happy, just as long as it is not at the cost of anybody else."

Mette Glargaard

Born in Denmark 1966, I had trouble complying with the default way of life. As an adult, I moved every few years, changed my job, changed partners – feeling ashamed that I couldn't settle down. In 2016 I discovered that it wasn't "couldn't", it was "wouldn't" and started my nomad life.

www.visiblehearts.com
www.facebook.com/BeingMette/
"Nothing is worth a struggle. It's okay to fight for something, but don't struggle. It's never worth it in the end. Hakuna matata!"

Katia Enbuske

Katia Enbuske is a world traveller and Digital Nomad. She's a professional business/life coach with a background in accounting, fitness, marketing, education and entrepreneurship. She has specialised in coaching people to achieve big dreams: becoming location independent, building their own business, changing jobs, studying a new profession, moving abroad or taking a break for travelling.

www.makeyourdreamhappen.com
"Live life to the fullest, right now, every day. Carpe diem."

Jan van Kuijk

Jan has been living partly in the Netherlands and partly in Hungary for more than 10 years. The two countries finally became too small for him and in 2018, after 15 years of preparation, he decided to travel the world as a Digital Nomad. With his work on WordPress and Joomla websites, he is generating sufficient income to live his dream.

https://digitalnomadlifestyle.nl/
https://janvankuijk.nl
"Live your dream, don't dream your life!"

Carolynne Alexander

Writer, speaker, coach and strategist for all things mission-driven and releasing your full potential. Armed with a master's degree in Business and Computing, Carolynne is a serial entrepreneur and lifelong learner with an obsession for championing mission-driven humans to build and lead successful businesses of the future.

carolynne.me (This is me, hola!)
themuseletter.co.uk (For weekly personal development and performance goodies.)
"Be an example of what's possible because you don't know who you're inspiring."

Dee Brooks

A mum of four adults, Dee is a passionate community development practitioner and trainer with over 20 years of experience. She has been an Intentional Nomad since 2015 and has travelled and worked in over 20 countries, creating impact through capacity building and knowledge sharing.

http://jeder.com.au
From a dream in Indonesia: "She never felt she fitted anywhere so she decided to fit everywhere."

Deborah Louise Botha

Debbie courageously leapt at the chance to travel and showcase her training development, coaching, negotiation and change-management skills within the world of cruising. She now wears officer stripes on her shoulders and a smile on her face as she explores international waters, is studying HR, dabbles in Bitcoin and revels in being a nurturing Nana.

linkedin.com/in/debbiebothaglobal
Instagram: @debbiebothaofficial
Jeremiah 29:11 – *"For I know the plans I have for you," declares the Lord, "plans to prosper you and not to harm you, plans to give you hope and a future."*

Michelle Clarke

Michelle Clarke is a global leadership coach who works with high-performing leaders and teams across the globe using the digital and virtual platform. Originally from South Africa, she is currently based in Santiago in Chile. Learn more about her work as a coach at www.motivcoach.com and her work as Portable Professional at www.portablepro.me. She is an avid yogi, photographer and stargazer.
"Keep Walking" thanks to Johnnie Walker Whiskey

Acknowledgements

A BOOK IS ALWAYS A team effort and I thrive being surrounded by people who become my extended heart family. I am deeply blessed to have an abundance of amazing people on my team – both for this book and in life!

Thanks to Mum, who is my pillar of support and endless unconditional love – sharing laughter, tears, soppy movies, wine and countless gallivants across the globe to meet me in some wonderful locations. In the past few years we have visited Spain, Greece (repeatedly), South Africa, Mauritius and the USA, and even survived three months of lockdown together in her home in the UK.

Megan – Your unconditional love and friendship blows me away. Heartfelt thanks to you, Rob and Nev for offering Stripey his forever home and laps to sprawl on.

Jemaja – for always offering your home as a safe refuge with cats to cuddle and *Masterclass*-type cuisine every single night. A chunk of this book unfolded in your home!

Sarah – my fabulous business partner lovingly known as "Wifey". Our connection is sacred. Working and laughing with writers while listening to heartfelt stories brings me such joy.

Nats – my unconditional soul sister. For #chaichats under the trees that birthed ideas to sell the IP of my business, to bendy yoga poses on sweaty carpets in India to farm walks in the Dale. RE!

My huge tribe of heart folk who each deserve an entire book. Your love, friendship and support over many years (some decades) keep me sane, grounded, laughing, vulnerable, safe and filled with pride to have you in my life. A note of thanks seems so ridiculously small when you are so huge in my life: Corlene, Brett, Bruce, Viki, Sandy, Patrick, Monique, Sarita, Richard, Nick, Gail, Nicole, Juanene, Debbie, Ven, Di R, Sue, Kath, Lynne, Hester, Colin, Di A, Ian, Daniela, Lynne L and Vincent.

ENP and family – for being my partner for most of this #LocationFree journey.

To the fabulous folk I met along the way – you breathe life into this book! You remind me that the generosity of the human spirit prevails, especially when you look for it! A special thanks to the 16 individuals who contributed to this book by sharing their experiences. In no particular order: Michelle Clarke, Dee Brooks, Victoria Watson, Carolynne Alexander, Jan van Kuijk, Katia Enbuske, Mette Glargaard, Deborah Botha, Nabila Welk, Gene Ellis, Uday Jhunjhunwala, Chris and Jillian de Cap, Martin van den Berg, Lynne Scullard, André Gussekloo and Nancy Benn. Your stories are truly inspirational.

Thanks, Sean, for coining my favourite term, #TeamLocationFree. Your professional eye and knowing you've "got my back" helps me relax. Thanks, too, to the rest of the team: Shannan, for the awesome illustration; Megan, for cover and design input; Clare, for expertise in the world of Amazon; Renate, for speedy transcriptions; Jen, for your kindness and eye; and Piet, for always being my photographer of choice.

Fellow writers, clients, friends and strangers all over the world for sharing "bum time", inspiration and feedback. You remind me what a privilege it is to dare to be an author. Particular thanks to the peeps in Malaga where the first draft of this book was written.

Thanks to all my Mastermind, retreat and coaching/de-cluttering clients who have been brave enough to work with me over the years. In particular, the YPO, which allowed me to travel and experience work in so many wonderful countries in true YPO style!

A final thanks to every space and place I have visited en route where the ideas and inspiration for this book were given wings. Every coffee shop, hotel room, veranda with spectacular views, every beach walked, mountain climbed, bicycle ridden, ferry caught, car hired, trainers worn and plane flown offered up a piece of this life I am living. Every kitty and dog that has given me a cuddle to make my heart smile and to miss my Stripey a little less.

The writing of this book happened because of you!

Thank you!